Purpose Revealed
Discovering Your Calling in the Midst of Trials

Jessica Smith

Published by Waldorf Publishing
2140 Hall Johnson Road
#102-345
Grapevine, Texas 76051
www.WaldorfPublishing.com

Purpose Revealed
Discovering Your Calling in the Midst of Trials

ISBN: 978-1-943276-99-8
Library of Congress Control Number: 2015957016

Copyright © 2016

All rights reserved. No part of this book may be reproduced or transmitted in any form or by any means whatsoever without express written permission from the author, except in the case of brief quotations embodied in critical articles and reviews. Please refer all pertinent questions to the publisher. All rights reserved. No part of this book may be reproduced or transmitted in any form or by any means, electronic or mechanical, including photocopying, recording, or by an information storage and retrieval system except by a reviewer who may quote brief passages in a review to be printed in a magazine or newspaper without permission in writing from the publisher.

Dedication

I am in awe that my Lord and Savior Jesus Christ would allow my journey to inspire others. This book has come to fruition only because of His goodness and favor. It's in Him that I live, move, and have my being. I asked the Lord to breathe motivation and encouragement onto every reader, and He has honored my request. He revealed to me how every trial was used to push me further into purpose. I am forever grateful and will use my life to bring Him glory.

To my Mother (Violine Jordan), Father (Henry Smith), Grandfather (the late Fred Jordan), and Grandmother (Annie Mae Jordan), you all raised me to love God and love people. There aren't enough words in any language to express how much I appreciate and love you all. You all have never told me anything to harm me, but only to better me. By my side is where you all remained throughout my entire journey. Your unwavering prayers were constant and effective. I LOVE YOU!

To Mr. and Mrs. Don Carey, you obeyed God by pushing and supporting this endeavor. I pray God's perpetual blessings over every aspect of your lives. THANK YOU!

To all of my family, friends, and supporters, I don't know where I would be without you. Your positive influence and impact have filled my world with joy. Thank you for listening and loving. Much love to you ALL!

Table of Contents

1. I'm Going to Tell…1
2. Lord, You Have to Help Me…21
3. Married to Ministry…42
4. He Knows What He's Doing…62
5. He Loves Me; He Loves Me Not…84
6. I've Been Dropped…103
7. How?!…117
8. What's Wrong With Me?...133
9. The Metamorphosis…153
   Author Bio…167

Purpose Revealed — Jessica Smith

Chapter 1: I'm Going to Tell

It was a sunny summer day. I can't remember the exact year, but I will never forget what happened. I went into the bathroom, and he came in and closed the door. I was caught off guard and wondered to myself what was happening. The bathroom wasn't very big, and he stood in front of the door. Then he reached into his pants and exposed the part of his body that made him a male. He said to me, "touch it." I told him *no*, yet he insisted again.

My Mother always told me not to let anyone touch my breasts or my private part. I can remember her telling me this as I was taking a bath. She said, "Jessica, if someone tries to touch you, then you kick, scream, and holler. If someone touches you, then come tell me." She drilled into my head that if someone violated me that it was not my fault and that I could always talk to her. Even at such an early age, she was reassuring me that no matter what happened to me that she would always be there for me.

As I stood in the bathroom on that summer day, the words of my beautiful Mother resonated within. I exclaimed, "if you don't let me out of this bathroom, I'm gonna scream and tell my Mama." It worked! He let me out of the bathroom. He attempted to steal my innocence, but I had been prepared for such a situation.

Purpose Revealed

Jessica Smith

    This is the first time that I recall feeling like a victim. His hopes of physically violating me were unsuccessful, but I still felt emotionally violated. I wondered "why me." I told no one! I was a young girl carrying a sizeable burden around. What did I do to bring this upon me? I know Mama said to, but should I tell? These are questions that I was pondering.

    It took a while, but eventually I told an older friend what happened. She encouraged me to tell my mother. I felt so ashamed. I felt so guilty. I knew that I didn't do anything wrong, but I felt as if I did. Having to verbally speak what happened brought all of these initial feelings back. I didn't know what the results of finally confiding in my mother would be. I remember feeling so dirty as I expressed to her what happened to me. Yet, I felt a burden lifted because I no longer had to carry this secret that I was too young to be lugging around. Immediately, my Grandfather, Grandmother, and Mom went to battle for me. Telling what transpired on that day was liberating.

    Silence gives power to hurt and pain. Revelation 12:11 (b) states, "And they have defeated him by the blood of the Lamb and by their testimony." Often, we are ashamed of our past and embarrassed by mistakes that we've made. Your test is a testimony that will help many, but you can't be ashamed to tell it. Your mess is a message that will lead to deliverance of the oppressed. Again, you have to tell it!

Looking back on my childhood experience revealed to me the significance of expression and communication. This reflection explains the reason I was drawn to the major of Speech Communication. I didn't know then that verbal communication would be fundamental to my career and calling. That negative situation positioned me to feeling a sense of empowerment after speaking truth. Now, I speak truth as I minister and am able to see the positive impact that it has on people.

According to Webster the word 'revealed' is defined as "no longer concealed; uncovered as by opening a curtain." The premise of this book is to share with you how all of the negativity, pain, loss, grief, misunderstandings, and rejection that I have faced pushed me into purpose. It was used to reveal what was already on the inside of me. Within all along was a minister, public speaker, life coach, author, and entrepreneur. But I didn't realize it until the pain pulled the cover off of who was hiding in me. As I share various storms that I've endured, I want you to look at your life and have what I like to call "revelation moments." It's those instances where you see what your personal adversity was teaching you, showing you, pulling out of you, and pushing you into. One of my favorite scriptures is Romans 8:28: "And we know that all things work together for good to them that love God, to them who are the called according to his purpose." What does the word all mean? It means ALL!

This means that the repossession, foreclosure, divorce, molestation, sickness, loss of your loved one, financial lack, loneliness, depression, mental illness, and every injurious situation that has come your way is actually working for you and not against you. Let's think of it in the terms of mathematics. If a negative number is multiplied by another negative number, it yields a positive number. So, the plethora of hardships that you've had to deal with are being used to unveil your purpose and to elevate you to a greater level.

The Safe Place

It is beneficial to your life to have a "safe place" that you can express hurtful situations. Surround yourself with those that truly have your best interest in mind. I have faced some really rough days, but what helped me was being able to send a text message or make a phone call to relieve myself of some of the thoughts going through my head. My spiritual sister, Pastor Robbie Cade Furdge, says "we don't fight alone." In other words, let your trusted support system know what's going on so they can help you. They can pray for you and be a sounding board to assist with solutions to your dilemma.

Of course, you can't trust everyone! Use discernment in choosing who to share your quandaries with. You may have a loved one that can aid in your emotional struggles because they've dealt with it and overcame it. Then you may have another friend that you can share a health crisis with, and they have the faith to hear the diagnosis, but decide to trust God for healing.

Also, in choosing your "safe place", be sure not to trust your innermost feelings with those that talk too much. If they will tell all of their business, then they will tell yours as well. If they are always discussing someone else's private issues, then yours will be added to their agenda as the next topic of discussion. Spend time in prayer asking God about who can be trusted and who can't. As my sweet Grandmother says, "Baby, you can't tell your business to everybody." Discernment is key!

After reading various articles about why men die earlier than women, it is often noted that a contributing factor is how men deal with stress. For all of the male readers, I want to emphasize the importance for you to verbalize and not internalize. Talk it out! Ask God to show you the person/persons that you can express to without condemnation. As you begin to verbalize your feelings, answers to your questions will come forth. When Jesus was in the Garden of Gethsemane, He felt like giving up. He was to bear the sins of the entire world. He had to bear every hurt, pain, disappointment, worry, discomfort, and discouragement that every person would ever experience. His excruciating, painful death was before him.

Purpose Revealed — Jessica Smith

'They went to the olive grove called Gethsemane, and Jesus said, "Sit here while I go and pray." He took Peter, James, and John with him, and he became deeply troubled and distressed. He told them, "My soul is crushed with grief to the point of death. Stay here and keep watch with me." He went on a little farther and fell to the ground. He prayed that, if it were possible, the awful hour awaiting him might pass him by. "Abba, Father," he cried out, "everything is possible for you. Please take this cup of suffering away from me. Yet, I want your will to be done, not mine' Mark 14:32-36 (NLT).

Do you think Jesus was stressed out? Definitely! He knew that His time of suffering had come. He was about to experience the betrayal of one of His disciples. He was about to endure a bloody death. The pressure of it all was just too much. The people that he loved would turn their backs on him. Yes, He is divine, but he was also in a human body. Although he never sinned, He was carrying the sins of the entire world. He was burdened. Luke's account (Luke 22:39-46) tells that his sweat was as drops of blood. He went to a place of prayer and took Peter, James, and John with him. When reading this passage of scripture, we often hurry to the part that Jesus is talking to His Father. I want to point out that before He began to talk to God that he expressed to Peter, James, and John that "My soul is crushed with grief to the point of death." He tells His inner circle what's going on with Him. He doesn't attempt to hide his sorrow from them, but He shares it with them and asks them to pray.

All of the data and statistics report that men outnumber women in death by suicide. This is due in part to a lack of expression. Men often suffer from depression in silence. The pressure that accompanies life can be overwhelming and a sense of hopelessness overtake them. To the male readers, I must emphasize the importance of finding your "safe place." Imitate the action of Jesus and express yourself. There are people close to you or that God is sending your way that will keep your feelings confidential, give wise counsel, and will pray for you. Do not be so tough that you miss out on the blessing of expression. If you need help, say it. If you love someone, tell them. It doesn't take away from your manhood at all to open up and communicate.

The Ultimate Safe Place

'When he had finished praying, Jesus left with his disciples and crossed the Kidron Valley. On the other side there was a garden, and he and his disciples went into it. Now Judas, who betrayed him, knew the place because Jesus had often met there with his disciples' John 18:1-2 (NLT).

After sharing with the disciples, Jesus then goes into prayer. He is telling the Father that he didn't want to go through what he was about to endure. His anxiety provoked him to give up. He's crying out to God for help. This is the "Ultimate Safe Place." Several scriptures (John 18:2, Luke 22:39) reveal to us that going to the Mount of Olives (Garden of Gethsemane) was not foreign to him. It was a place of communication because he took His disciples with Him there. It was a place of prayer and meditation. Judas knew he could find Him there because he, himself, was there as a disciple as Jesus taught them there. He escorted those that sought to take the life of Jesus there because it was a place where Jesus was known to be at. Judas, the betrayer, knew that Jesus could be found in a place of prayer.

When facing adversity, where can you be found? When dealing with tedious circumstances, what's your location? I'm not speaking just geographically, but spiritually to the posture that you assume. There is strength administered to you in prayer. Tactics and strategies for overcoming are downloaded into your spirit when you lay before God. 1 Peter 5:8 states, "Stay alert! Watch out for your great enemy, the devil. He prowls around like a roaring lion, looking for someone to devour." When the nemesis comes for you, let him find you the way Judas found Jesus; in the place of prayer. It may feel like it, but you will not be defeated. At times, it feels as if the enemy's advances seem to be working against your health, family, finances, business endeavors, relationships, resources, connections, emotions, etc. Let me issue a friendly reminder that you are more than a conqueror. One of my favorite statements is "we always win." When it looks like defeat, you will come out victorious. Even if you take a loss, what you gain is going to be greater than what you lost. This level of resolve comes through prayer. I'm not speaking of every once in a while prayer, I'm referencing constant communication with God.

Jesus' prayer in the Garden of Gethsemane was heartfelt and sincere. He expressed to the Lord that He didn't want to go through what He was about to face. Prayer to the Father is the "ultimate safe place." It's the place where you can say "God, I don't understand." It's the place where you can admit that you feel like giving up. It's the place that you can lay before Him and say "God, I just need you to help me." It's in prayer that you can cry out "God, I don't want to be like this." You are safe in His arms!

In my home, I have a particular spot that I lay out a certain quilt and lay before God. I call it my altar. Many days my heart was so broken that all I could do was crawl out of bed and lay on what I deemed to be my personal altar. I can remember crying until my face was swollen. I recall hurting so bad that I physically felt ill. My tears saturated the quilt. Often times, I was in the fetal position, and all I could say was God please help me. I now reflect on those moments and realize that in those instances of helplessness that God gave me power and strength through prayer.

After Jesus had expressed Himself to His closest disciples and to the Father, His resolve was strengthened. It was after this that He drew the conclusion to let the Father's will be done regardless of how He felt.

Change Your Perspective

I remember watching the Manny Pacquiao vs. Floyd Mayweather boxing match at a fight party. I'm certainly not a boxing connoisseur, but would watch fights with my Grandfather while growing up. I never knew a lot about the sport, but I enjoyed watching it. My Grandfather was a boxer in his younger years, so he loved it. He had an understanding of the sport that I didn't possess. So here I am years later viewing this fight and thinking that I have the same level of comprehension as my Grandfather. As I'm watching the fight, I'm seeing Pacquiao land punches and blocking them. In between snack breaks (the food was good) I was back in front of the big screen TV watching these two boxers go at it. In my eyes, Pacquiao was winning and was going to win. Well, he didn't. I realized that I viewed Mayweather in a negative light which caused me not to cheer for him. Pacquiao, on the other hand, was a bold Christian, and He was giving God the glory for his success. He spoke of how the Lord changed him. His story was so inspiring to me. I was elated to see someone using a major platform to give glory to our Creator. My favorable view of Pacquiao led me to want him to win. He was losing, and I didn't know it because of my lack of proper comprehension of the sport of boxing and my positive view of him.

    I'm a New Orleans Saints fan! Always have been and always will be. My Mother has Saints flags for her car and Saints floor mats. So, it's a generational love that we have for "Who Dat" Nation. I went to a game where we (yes, I said we) played the undefeated Carolina Panthers. It was one of the best games I've witnessed. The Superdome was blazing! The season hadn't been so great for the Saints, but giving the Panthers their first loss was apparently on the mind of the Saints players. There was a catch made by the opposing team that was questionable. My friend leaned over to ensure that I had the insight of the rule that the ground cannot assist in the catch. While the referees were reviewing the play, it was being shown on the screens throughout the Dome. All of the Saints fans around me were saying that it wasn't a catch, and I agreed with them. All of the Carolina Panthers fans were exclaiming the opposite. Because of my devotion to the Saints, I saw the play from a perspective different than that of the Panthers fans.

Culture, past experiences, the way an individual was raised, what they are currently dealing with, and other factors impact their perception. The mind looks at a situation and takes many variables into place and draws a conclusion. This is why two people can hear the same conversation and come away with two totally different accounts of what happened. They can both hear the exact same words being spoken, but their perception shapes their opinions of what happened.

Over the years, I've learned to change my perspective. Even though a man attempted to molest me and steal my innocence, I choose to see that situation differently now than I did before. The sight of him used to make me cringe. To think about it would make me uncomfortable. Now, I understand that circumstance was used to teach me the power of expression and using my voice. I was terrified to tell. Even though my Mother told me that I could talk to her about anything, I found myself voiceless. After telling and releasing the burden I was carrying, I felt a sense of security because my family went to bat for me. My Mother, Grandmother, and Grandfather made sure that I felt safe, protected, and loved. I gained from it the ability to understand that my voice has power. I can speak, and things will happen. My expressiveness was of benefit to me. Sharing this information was the first difficult conversation that I can remember. It prepped me to handle with poise future problematic situations.

It is up to you to change your own perception. Instead of focusing on the negative emotions that are connected to trials that you've faced, extract from it the lesson and the blessing. Change the way you see the divorce. Change the way you see the bankruptcy. Change the way you see the financial hardship. Change the way you see the rape or molestation. Change the way you see the illness. Don't miss out on all of the good that's to come out of the bad stuff. Never allow damaging situations to continue causing you harm. It happened so take authority over your view and modify your perception. There are people who have gone through more than you and still thrived. On the other hand, there are those who could never handle what you've endured. It's a matter of choice!

Let's pause for a brief exercise. Think of three adverse situations that you have dealt with or are currently dealing with and list them below:

1._____
2._____
3._____

Now, list the lesson and blessing that you are choosing to see in the above listed adverse situations:

1. Lesson:_____
   Blessing:_____
2. Lesson:_____
   Blessing:_____
3. Lesson:_____
   Blessing:_____

The way a situation is viewed has the ability to affect its outcome. At the Saints game that I attended, the referees ruled the debatable play as a catch. This positioned the Panthers down the field and allowed them to get closer to their goal of achieving a touchdown. They ended up winning the game. Allow every hurt, wound, mistake, setback, disappointment, and failure to position you to achieve a metaphorical touchdown in life.

The well-known actor Sidney Poitier reportedly hit a bump in the road early in his career. He was told by the casting director after an audition, "Why don't you stop wasting people's time and go out and become a dishwasher or something." He could have taken the rejection and let it discourage him to the point that he decided never to try again. He could have given up on his aspirations. He could've viewed his dismissal as an indicator that his dreams were too big for a poor, black man from the Bahamas. Poitier went on to become the first African American to win an Academy Award for Best Actor. He has received numerous honors and awards. In 2009, he was awarded the Presidential Medal of Freedom by President Barack Obama. His setback became a set up for him to become one of the greatest actors in history.

1 Thessalonians 5:18 states, "In every thing give thanks: for this is the will of God in Christ Jesus concerning you." This is one of my favorite encouraging scriptures. It is a reminder that we are to be thankful in every situation. Whether joyful or tearful, aching or well, wealthy or wanting, we are to be grateful. Thanksgiving is one of my favorite holidays because during this time people are pausing and focusing on their blessings. The less-fortunate are being fed and volunteers aid at homeless shelters. It is extremely beneficial to you mentally to reflect on all that you have to be appreciative of. The enemy will often magnify your problems. The adversary will take extreme measures and use people to keep anguishes on your mind. Your perspective will change when you decide to tap into thankfulness. Allow yourself to mature to the point that you are able to give God thanks for trusting you with the hardships that have come.

In January 2015, Pastor Buddy Peters made his transition from earth to Glory. He and his wife (Sis. Debra Peters) are partially responsible for my success. After his passing, I thought about how I was not ready for him to be gone. I wanted to get his advice on some things in my life. He was a Father-figure, and I was in no way prepared for his departure. Then, it hit me! I thought about how he always kept a microphone in my hand. He would often speak to my destiny and tell me that I was going to be great. He told me how proud he was of me the day that he presented my license to preach the Gospel. He was a progressive man and a forward thinker. He was never afraid to step out on faith. Pastor was a trendsetter and trailblazer. I watched him leave dialysis and still come and minister to God's people. Even when he was in pain, you couldn't beat him praising God. As I began to reflect on all of this, I couldn't help but say "Thank you, God." His life impacted mine and too many people to ever count. It was a painful loss, but as I began to think of the many lessons and blessings that came from his life my heart was filled with joy.

Fact vs. Truth

'And Caleb stilled the people before Moses, and said, Let us go up at once, and possess it; for we are well able to overcome it. [31] But the men that went up with him said, we be not able to go up against the people; for they are stronger than we. [32] And they brought up an evil report of the land which they had searched unto the children of Israel, saying, the land, through which we have gone to search it, is a land that eateth up the inhabitants thereof; and all the people that we saw in it are men of a great stature.

[33] And there we saw the giants, the sons of Anak, which come of the giants: and we were in our own sight as grasshoppers, and so we were in their sight' (Numbers 13: 30-33).

Moses was instructed by the Lord to send out 12 spies to survey Canaan. The land was promised to the Children of Israel. God had been so faithful that they had absolutely no reason to doubt Him. As they are spying out the land, they see the descendants of Anak there. These are giants that were occupying the land. They discover that the land is bountiful and productive. They discover that the land is flowing with milk and honey. Yet 10 of the 12 come back with an evil report out of fear of the giants. They told the people that they saw themselves as grasshoppers compared to the giants and that the giants saw them that way as well. They stated that they couldn't possess the land because the people there were stronger than them. The ones that said we can't were not allowed to enter the Promised Land. Only Joshua and Caleb, who spoke up and said that we are well able to overcome made it in. You shall have what you say! Don't talk yourself out of the blessings that you have been pre-approved for.

It was a fact that there were giants in the land. The truth is that God gave them the land and all they had to do was possess it. It was a fact that the people there were stronger than them. The truth is that they had the backing of the God of the Universe. John 14:6 states, Jesus told him, "I am the way, the TRUTH, and the life. No one can come to the Father except through me." Choose truth over facts! A cancer diagnosis from the doctor is the fact. The Word, which states, "by His stripes we are healed," is the truth. Dealing with depression is the fact, but the truth is that the joy of the Lord is your strength. The fact is that everything around you may seem to be going crazy, but the truth is that God will give peace that surpasses all understanding. Acknowledge the fact, but speak the truth. Change what you say and you will eventually change what you see.

Out of all the things that God could've used to create the world, He chose words. He said let there be light and there was light. He spoke the sun, moon, waters, and animals into existence. God could have waved His hand and everything would've come forth. The account of creation teaches us about speaking authority. We see God speaking and seeing what He spoke.

And God said, "Let us make man in our image, after our likeness: and let them have dominion over the fish of the sea, and over the fowl of the air, and over the cattle, and over all the earth, and over every creeping thing that creepeth upon the earth. [27] So God created man in his own image, in the image of God created he him; male and female created he them" (Genesis 1:26-27 KJV).

Purpose Revealed   Jessica Smith

Throughout Genesis 1 it states, "God said let there be." After He created male and female, we see no more "Let there be's," because He gave dominion to them. He allowed man to have speaking authority like Him. He created man in His image and likeness. For example, I look like my Mother. I have some of her personality traits because I came from her. Man and woman were given God-like qualities and characteristics. He gave them authority and rights to rule over the earth. Adam was given the responsibility to name the animals and whatever he called them is what we still call them today. Once Jesus Christ is received into the heart, it puts us back in the original fellowship that Adam and Eve had with God. We get our dominion back.

Your words have power. That's why you must be extremely careful with the words that you release into the atmosphere. The world that you live in now is a direct reflection of what you've been speaking. If you continue to say I'm broke, then that's what you will be. If you continue to speak negativity, then that is what you will see. Again, I say when you change what you say you will change what you see. If you don't like what you see, then use your God-given authority and speak to it. Decree the Word of God over your children. Don't call them bad or degrade them. Speak truth to them and their future. Decree that no matter how it appears that they will be great. All of my life, my

Grandmother told me that I can do whatever I put my mind to. Her words of affirmation are manifested every time I preach or host an event to empower and strengthen others. Declare that you are the head and not the tail; above and not beneath. Declare that you are more than a conqueror. Declare that no matter how difficult the situation you face that you will always come out victorious. Confess that you are smart enough to pursue that next level degree. Confess that you will be all that God has called for you to be. Confess that you have everything that you need to launch the business. Decree that you are out of debt and all of your needs are met. Decree that your family is healthy, wealthy, wise, and restored. Decree that your Nation is improving. Decree that you will not let fear keep you from instituting programs that will aid the less fortunate.

    The Scripture states in Proverbs 18:21 that the power of death and life are in the tongue. No more will you nonchalantly speak that which will cause you or others harm. After being equipped with this information, you will decree, declare, confess, and profess life to every dead area of your life. Remember, you shall have what you say!

Chapter 2: Lord, You Have to Help Me

I was sixteen years old, and my sweet Grandfather was in the hospital in Hattiesburg, MS. He had been battling cancer like a trooper. He was placed in a large room on the end because our family is so large. He and my Grandmother had nine children. All of them have children, and some have grandchildren. I didn't know that Paw Paw was as sick as he was. I witnessed him being hospitalized before and bounce back. The way I figured out that his situation was so terminal was when my cousin Edward got upset. I knew for cool, manly Edward to be so affected that this situation had to be worse than I was made aware of. At this point, my head is spinning. I'm thinking: *is my Paw Paw about to die*. This is the man that raised me and taught me how to drive. He taught me how to count money. When my mother and grandmother scolded me, he is who I ran to for comfort. He would say, "Now you've got to act right."

In my eyes, the greatest man to walk the earth after Jesus was Mr. Fred Jordan. Everybody knew my Paw Paw. He was so kind and friendly. He was rather smooth and well-dressed. He was laid back and didn't raise his voice. He had a voice that reminded me of Al Green. I can remember going to church and him always being called up to sing a solo. I was so pleased to see him up singing and the audience taking in every note that he belted out. I was

Mr. Fred's grandbaby and proud to be. He would play tapes on his radio in his room. I would go in with him to practice a song that I had to sing, and he would give me advice. He said, "You don't have to sing it just like them. Make the song your own." He is still known for singing certain songs, but the one that stands out the most to me is "Remind Me Dear Lord."

The things that I love and hold dear to my heart
are just borrowed they're not mine at
all Jesus only let me use them to brighten my life
So remind me, remind me, dear Lord

Roll back the curtain of memory now and then
Show me where you brought me from
And where I could have been
Remember I'm human, and humans forget
So remind me, remind me, dear Lord

Nothing good have I done to deserve God's own Son
I'm not worthy of the scars in his hands
Yet he chose the road to Calvary to die in my stead
Why he loved me, I can't understand

Roll back the curtain of memory now and then
Show me where you brought me from
And where I could have been
Remember I'm human, and humans forget
So remind me, remind me, dear Lord.

He told me that when he saw my grandmother that she was the prettiest woman that he ever laid eyes on. He was willing to do whatever it took to make Miss Annie Mae McCoy his lady. He saw what he wanted and went after it. He made that beautiful young woman his wife and built a family that God is proud of. They lived in the projects and struggled financially at times raising nine children. He worked hard and endured racism in the small town of Poplarville, MS to make sure that his wife and children were taken care of. His hard work paid off, and he built our family a home in which I was raised.

One year for Easter, he brought home for me a rabbit. A real live rabbit! Periodically, he would pop up with candy or something sweet for me. I watched him love my grandmother and how he attended to her after her brother David Ray McCoy was killed. I observed how he straightforwardly, yet lovingly dealt with family issues. He had the ability to calm any situation down. What's that in the sky? Is it a bird? Is it a plane? No, it's Paw Paw to the rescue. He was my real life superhero!

It is January 1998, and we are in the hospital, and my Paw Paw is on his death bed. I walked into an empty room and leaned on the bed. I took a minute to process everything, and it was difficult to entertain the thought that our family was about to lose our patriarch. My heart was sorrowful, and I cried tears of sadness. Then, I prayed. I told the Lord, "If you are going to take my Grandfather, then you are going to have to help me. I can't make it through this without You." In that moment, I knew that I needed strength beyond my own to say goodbye to the man that raised me, defended me, protected me, loved me, taught me, embraced me, communicated with me, respected me, and valued me.

That evening some of my first cousins and I were instructed by our parents to go to my Uncle Willie's and Aunt Gail's house, take a bath, and prepare for bed. We were told that if anything happened that they would call us. We followed their instructions. As we were settling down, we received a phone call to come back to the hospital. My cousin Nicole was driving my Mom's Honda Accord and was speeding to get us back to find out what's going on with our Paw Paw. I'll never forget the sorrow that saturated the atmosphere when we walked into the room. By looking at the faces of my aunts, uncles, and my loving Grandmother, I knew that Paw Paw was gone. He wasn't just staying at the hospital for a few days this time. He was not gone for a little while to take grandmother to Chicago to visit her brothers and sisters. He was gone… forever! How would life ever be the same for our family? How could I go home and walk into his room and he not be there? Whose lap would I lay my head in to fall asleep like I did his?

In retrospect, I realize that the loss of my Grandfather taught me about the power of prayer and how to handle grief. At some point, everyone experiences grief. It could be due to the death of a loved one or the loss of a long-term friendship. It could be caused by divorce or a child going away to jail. No matter its origin, the pain associated with it is real. His transition to Heaven taught me how to keep living after loss. As you continue to read the book, you will see that this was a lesson that I needed to learn for trials to come. In the time of mourning, I cried out to God, and He helped me. He gave me strength. He gave me hope. He gave me the endurance to move forward.

Let me serve as a witness that if you cry out to your Heavenly Father for help, that He will certainly be there for you. I didn't say that He will change the situation, but He will change your outlook of it. He didn't bring my Grandfather back but allowed me to see all of the good that he served while on earth and how I benefited from being raised by him. He allowed me to see that my faith in Him was increased because He was with me in my grief.

What Does Grief Look Like

Dr. Elizabeth Kubler-Ross is a Swiss-born psychiatrist that is well-known for her studies of death and grief. In 1969, she released a book entitled "On Death and Dying" where she outlines the five emotional stages associated with death. Her study is based upon conversations with terminally ill patients at the University of Chicago. Her dialogue with those that received news of their impending death gives insight into the experience of receiving devastating news. Dr. Kubler-Ross didn't set out to do a study on grief and bereavement, but her observations have been adopted by many as the five stages of grief. The stages aren't listed concurrently, and some stages may be skipped. The Kubler-Ross Model outlines five possible stages: Denial, Anger, Bargaining, Depression, and Acceptance. Let's look at each stage separately and utilize it to help gain an understanding of grievous responses.

Denial

"The first reaction to learning of terminal illness or death of a cherished loved one is to deny the reality of the situation. It is a normal reaction to rationalize overwhelming emotions. It is a defense mechanism that buffers the immediate shock. We block out the words and hide from the facts. This is a temporary response that carries us through the first wave of pain."

My Uncle, Elder Darryl Jordan, was once on drugs and now he ministers to those overcoming addiction. His substance abuse caused him to hit rock bottom. His lifestyle was problematic, and everyone knew that he was on "that stuff." It was clear to all except his Mother. My grandmother was the last to finally accept the fact that her baby boy was strung out on drugs. It was her coping mechanism to deny it. She and my grandfather raised their children in church, so that's not how they were expected to turn out. She didn't want to admit it, but eventually acknowledged his dire state.

Through my Uncle's drug addiction, he found purpose. He gave his life to Christ and has been clean since that point. He personally ministers to those that are facing the struggle that once disabled him. He's gone into prisons sharing his testimony and has seen many people set free. He has also ministered his story at rehabilitation centers and witnessed the chains of addiction be destroyed. Purpose was revealed in an ugly situation.

Anger

"Anger can present itself in a variety of ways—anger at your loved one, at others, at God, at the world, at yourself. And anger can be a difficult emotion to cope with. Some will express anger easily and toward anyone or anything, but many of us will suppress the anger instead, keeping it bottled up or even turning it inward, toward ourselves. Anger turned inward is guilt—guilt that we "should have done something," or even guilt that we feel angry toward the deceased. But anger is a natural response to loss. And if we're able to identify and label our anger, it

can help us express it in healthier ways that don't hurt others or ourselves. Saying, "I'm angry," and letting yourself feel that anger is part of the healing process."

I have a friend that experienced the loss of his parents within a short period of time. He lost his father first and then his mother became sick. He stood by her side. I can remember being on the phone when he entered into her hospital room and how he lovingly greeted her. I could hear how his voice shifted on the days that she wasn't doing so well. She was sick, and her condition was growing worse, but he prayed for her healing. He believed that she would be raised up and restored to health. She received her ultimate healing by joining her husband in Heaven.

My friend later expressed to me that he had been depressed and angry with God. He's a minister that prays for others and has seen God perform miracles at his petition. Yet, he felt that God let him down by allowing his mother to leave earth. I was shocked because I didn't know that he had been dealing with such an emotion toward the God that we both serve and trust. He was mad with the God that we prayed to and dedicated our lives to. I felt a sense of guilt for not previously knowing that he had been struggling emotionally on such an intense level. My view of him as a strong Man of God caused me to miss it.

Since the passing of his Mother, he has been granted the opportunity to serve in full-time ministry. It is my belief that if she were still alive that he would not have left his job and ventured into an unknown territory and geographic area. It was her death that pushed him into purpose. His dealing with and conquering his greatest emotional dilemma strengthened his relationship with God. He now trusts God whether it makes sense or not. His increased comprehension of the sovereignty of God is now blessing hundreds on a weekly basis.

Bargaining
"With bargaining, there's a sense that we just want life back to the way it used to be. We wish we could go back in time, catch the illness sooner, see something we didn't see. We may also feel guilty, focusing on "If only…" Bargaining can begin before the loss occurs or after. If the death or loss was anticipated, such as in the case of illness, bargaining may have been going on for a while—we bargain with God to please "spare" our loved one; we say we'll "do anything" to keep them here. If the death or loss was sudden, we may wish we could bring them back or go back in time and change things. Bargaining keeps us focused on the past, so we don't have to feel the emotions of the present."

I was working as a Property Manager of a 432 unit apartment community. Many mornings I came early and most of the time left late. The property was a property that faced many challenges. Occupancy was down, and illegal activity was up. I faced issues with staffing and finances. I was told to avoid business owners that had been waiting past the grace period for their invoices to be paid. In spite of the issues, I worked to improve the property. I instituted a Community Watch Program to help with crime. The tenants were encouraged to anonymously leave notes to report prohibited practices in the rent drop box. I cracked down on non-rent payers and personally dealt with tenant issues. One of the regional managers left a note that stated: "You are turning this property into the jewel that we know it can be."

One day out of the blue and without warning, individuals from the corporate office came in and terminated me. They stated that they felt like a different type of manager was needed. No warning, no coaching, and not much assistance from them was given. I told them "It's ok because God will take care of me." I said that, but at the same time was nervous about this sudden loss of income. I started thinking about the what if's. I played the termination conversation over and over in my head. At one point, I started wanting the money back that I was making so badly.

It wasn't long after they unjustly fired me that the company filed for bankruptcy. This revealed God to be as my Defender. I didn't have to degrade them or discourage others from leasing from them. It was a college apartment community, and I was over a college ministry at the time with well over 100 students. I had the ability to denigrate that company but chose not to. I'm glad I didn't because I maintained my integrity and witnessed God being the Judge over the situation. While dealing with the grief of losing a nice salary, God was revealed to me as Defender and Provider.

Depression

"This stage of grief occurs in some people after they realize the true extent of the loss. Signs of depression may include sleep and appetite disturbances, a lack of energy and concentration, and crying spells. A person may feel loneliness, emptiness, isolation, and self-pity."

I thought that he was the love of my life. After surviving divorce and dating a few nice guys, I thought the Lord had sent an angel in bodily form to love me. From the very beginning, our conversations were deep and intense. We would talk for hours about everything. I always thought that my eyes were dark brown until he told of how on our first date the candlelight showed their lighter brown hue. He made me a better person. He opened up and told me his story, and I felt safe enough to share mine. We would often say to each other, "Where have you been all of my life," and "I've never known a love like this." There's more to this story! In a later chapter, it's discussed in more detail.

As you can imagine, the breakup was devastating to me. I lost weight because my appetite was affected. When I was asleep, I would have dreams about him. It was more difficult than the divorce because I opened up, trusted again, and was devastated again. Some days it felt as if I cried enough tears to fill up the Mississippi River. I was depressed!

In the midst of the hurt, I kept preaching and teaching. I kept counseling and advising. I learned how to press past the pain and continue to operate in purpose. I learned that I was stronger than I ever knew. While facing the disappointment, I met other young ladies that were dealing with the grief of a romantic relationship failure. I had a "revelation moment" while speaking to a young lady that was going through a divorce. I realized that this was a part of my ministry. Helping hurting women is a branch of my purpose that I can operate in with empathy and understanding. The pain pushed me further into purpose.

<u>Acceptance</u>

"Many people mistakenly believe that "acceptance" means we are "cured" or "alright" with the loss. But this isn't the case at all. The loss will forever be a part of us though we will feel it more some times than others.

Purpose Revealed — Jessica Smith

Acceptance simply means we are ready to try and move on—to accommodate ourselves to this world without our loved one. This process can actually bring us closer to the one we loved as we make sense of how life was and process how we want life now to be."

My goddaughter, Tomeka, received a diagnosis of Multiple Sclerosis. She was being seen by various doctors, and her health issues seemed to be a mystery. She would have days that she was in so much physical pain that it affected her mobility. At times, this young woman in her 30s needed the assistance of a walker to get around. One morning she called and exclaimed, "Mama, I can't move." I could hear complete terror in her voice. This led to yet another trip to the Emergency Room.

Tomeka's ministry is connected to movement. The liturgical dance ministry (Worshipping Warriors) that she is a part of is often called upon to assist church services, events, and conferences. Can you imagine her frustration? Her condition affects her passion. She's had to sit on the sidelines while her fellows go forth in dance. Psalm 150:4 (a) states to praise the Lord in timbrel and dance. She went through schooling and endured training to ensure that she honored this scripture in excellence.

As we were conversing one day, she stated: "I asked the Lord to heal me, but if He doesn't I still say yes." It was such a proud moment for me. She has endured more heartache, pain, and sickness than anybody that I know. To hear her embrace the situation, but face it with determination was like music to my ears. Her motivation to accept the situation, yet persevere through it stimulated my faith. The situation didn't change, but her outlook on it did.

God's Choice is dance school that Tomeka has launched since her diagnosis. It is a mentorship program that is correspondence in nature to assist those that feel a call to dance ministry. She has instituted her education, instruction, and experience to equip others with the knowledge to operate effectively. As she was in bed and having difficulty moving one day, the idea came. A deeper level of purpose was revealed through the disease.

Jesus Grieved Too

The account of Jesus in the Garden of Gethsemane shows us some of Dr. Kubler-Ross' grief observations. Jesus is about to die and expresses His piercing sorrow to the disciples. Luke's account tells of sweat falling like drops of blood from Him. He exhibits signs of depression. His anguish is clearly observed. The others fall asleep, but He's up praying to His Father. In addition to depression, we see bargaining. He asks the Father that if there is another way to do this, possibly that route could be considered. He understands that His purpose is to die for the sins of the world, but in this moment of grief requests a way out of the pain. Lastly, we see Jesus' acceptance of His fate. He states, "Yet not my will, but yours be done."

As Jesus prepares for the pain, suffering, and death that is before Him, we find Him praying. It is through prayer that he gains the strength needed for what's about to take place. It must be noted, that He didn't wait until this moment to activate the tool of prayer. His prayer life is documented throughout the New Testament. Luke 11:1 states, "And it came to pass, that, as He was praying in a certain place, when He ceased, one of His disciples said unto Him, Lord, teach us to pray, as John also taught his disciples." Many quote the Lord's Prayer, but this scripture reveals to us that prior to teaching it to the disciples that He had been in prayer. Luke 6:12-13 says, "And it came to pass in those days, that He went out into a mountain to pray, and continued all night in prayer to God. And when it was the day, He called unto Him His disciples: and of them, he chose twelve, whom also he named apostles." Here we see Jesus praying all night long before choosing those that will walk closely with Him in His work on earth. Jesus clearly had an understanding of the power of prayer. Because of His consistent prayer life, it's not a surprise that in His most distressful time that He's found in a place of prayer.

Much Prayer Much Power

Prayer doesn't just change things. It changes everything! The Bible tells us that we are to "pray without ceasing." This means we should remain in prayer mode to the point that it becomes our response and reaction. In certain instances, I've received news and picked up the phone and shared the information with my Mother or friends. After discussing it, the situation was still present. After talking about it, my feelings were unadjusted. When I presented the circumstance to God in prayer, I came out with a new perspective. In prayer, my view of the situation began to shift. There is an empowerment that takes place in prayer. Never engage in discourse with others more than you do you Heavenly Father about something that is troubling. Within prayer are all of the answers to the questions that we have, but it's up to us to extract them. Let's look at just a few benefits of prayer…

"Listen to my voice in the morning, Lord. Each morning I bring my requests to You and wait expectantly" (Psalm 5:3).

Expectancy is refreshed in prayer. You may be in a place of hopelessness, but as you speak to the Father, your expectation will be revived. It's a miserable life to live not expecting anything. Optimism and positivity will spring forth. I've entered into prayer feeling defeated and left out saying, "It won't always be like this." Although my trial remained, I began to anticipate victory. As you pray, expect to see results. Expect breakthrough. Expect enlightenment. Expect solutions. Expect change.

    Your Father desires to talk to you. Remember prayer is not a monologue, but a dialogue. It's you making your requests known, but also a time for Him to speak to you. How would you feel if someone calls you, says everything that they want to say, and hangs up? During prayer, pause and seek to hear God. He will speak to your spirit. Expect to hear His voice. Ask Him for guidance. Ask Him for direction. Anticipate answered prayers.

    In the above-referenced scripture, it says, "Each morning I bring my requests." This means that the author had a routine. There's no better way to start the day than with prayer. Schedule a daily appointment with the Master. You should find yourself praying throughout the day, but your private devotion time will prove beneficial to your entire well-being. When an appointment is made with a specialty physician, that appointment typically doesn't get canceled because his/her schedule may be filled for months. The Great Physician has time for you and gives you the liberty to set your appointments with Him. He desires to hear from you as much as possible. He also has pertinent information that He will speak to you in the private time with Him.

"The righteous cry out, and the Lord hears them; He delivers them from all their troubles. The Lord is close to the brokenhearted and saves those who are crushed in spirit. The righteous person may have many troubles, but the Lord delivers him from them all." Psalm 34:17-19

Another benefit of prayer is that it yields deliverance. God is mighty and powerful. He created humans with organs, muscles, tissues, and joints. He created the blue sky and green grass. The multiplicity of animals was fashioned when spoken into existence. The Word tells us that if we cry out to God that He WILL deliver us. What an assurance to know that we can cry out to God, and He hears us. It can be very frustrating to speak to someone, and they pay you no attention. You can be pouring out your heart, and they express no concern. It's aggravating to feel like what you are sharing with someone is important, and they are distracted or demonstrating a lack of focus. Not only does He hear us, but He has the power to get us out of trouble. It doesn't say that we won't have trouble. It actually alludes to the fact that the righteous may experience many troubles, but we have a Deliverer. We have help in the midst of the storm. As you cry to Him, expect deliverance.

I've suffered more disappointments than I can count. I've had my heart broken. I've been lied to and lied about. My checking account has been in the red more than a few times. I've had disease in my body. I've been mistreated

Purpose Revealed   Jessica Smith

and abused. I've gone through a public divorce. I've faced infertility. All of this happened after I gave my life to Christ. Throughout all of it, I prayed. Sometimes very short prayers like "Lord, help." I would be dishonest if I allowed you to believe that I was perfect and always full of faith. I messed up and made mistakes. Yet, I would say things like "Lord, I need You to help me." At times, I was so confused and thought to myself that this Jesus stuff is no longer working for me. Yet, I would find myself crying out to Him again. No matter what I faced, He kept delivering me. He kept making a way for me. He continued to bless. God allowed me to be a partaker of his grace and mercy even when I know that I didn't deserve it. He loved me when I didn't love myself. I prayed even when I didn't feel like it. You may have troubles all around, go pray about it and stand in expectation of your deliverance.

"But to Hannah he gave a double portion because he loved her, and the Lord had closed her womb. Because the Lord had closed Hannah's womb, her rival kept provoking her in order to irritate her….. [10] Hannah was in deep anguish, crying bitterly as she prayed to the Lord…..[20] So in the course of time Hannah became pregnant and gave birth to a son. She named him Samuel, saying Because I asked the Lord for him," I Samuel 1:5-6, 10, 20.

Results are manifested through prayer. In 1 Samuel Chapter 1, we have the account of Hannah. She was barren and longed for a child. She specifically asked the Lord for a man child. As was customary during this time, her husband had another wife. The other wife, Peninnah, had children and exasperated Hannah's sorrow by making fun of her not being able to bear children. I noticed that we don't see Hannah retaliating or being vengeful. Her humbleness showed when she was in the Temple praying to God for a child, and Prophet Eli accused her of being drunk. She politely tells him that she's not inebriated, but what her request is that she's brought to God in prayer. The Prophet says to her "Go in peace, and may the God of Israel grant you what you have asked of him."

When Hannah leaves from praying at the Temple, her countenance changes. She is no longer downcast or long-faced. Her appetite returns. Her expectancy is rejuvenated, and deliverance from the irritation caused by Peninnah has transpired. She doesn't have a baby bump yet. She's not holding a child, but something happened in prayer that assures her that there will soon be a display of God's Word.

Whatever you ask God for in prayer that aligns with His Word, believe it and receive it. Stop doubting and second-guessing. When you exit your time of prayer, leave knowing that it is handled. As a matter of fact, start positioning yourself to possess the blessings that you've requested from God. Before you proceed with reading, I admonish you to pause and think about what you've been believing God for. Now, give Him the praise for it like it's already done!

After they get home, guess what happens? Hannah becomes intimate with her husband. Keep in mind, that manifestation requires participation. No matter what she prayed, if she didn't position herself to be impregnated by her husband, then she would've remained childless. You may have dreams and aspirations of owning a business. Begin to formulate the business plan. Maybe you are asking God for a spouse. Start to prepare yourself for marriage.

Hannah becomes the mother of the Prophet Samuel. Her results are the fruit of prayer. Instead of complaining, pray. Your desired results are just a prayer away!

Chapter 3: Married to Ministry

It was June 1999, and I had recently graduated from high school. I attended a church service with my cousins. In church, I noticed this nice looking guy with a plaid Polo shirt and nice khakis on. After service, he came up to me and asked if I was saved and I replied yes. Next he asked if I had a boyfriend and I replied no. He introduced himself to me and asked for my telephone number. Cell phones weren't as popular then, and I didn't have one yet, so I gave him my home number. He wrote my name and number on the first page of his brown Bible.

I stayed with my cousins that night and went to my home the next day. My Mother informed me that I had missed a call from a young man. It was him! When we talked, we had the best conversation. We talked for a long while. He told me about his daughter and that she was three years old. I was only 18 and was nervous to tell my mom and grandma that he had a child. I was impressed because, in our initial conversation, she was mentioned very early in our dialogue. I respected him for her being of such importance to him that she was a priority discussion.

It wasn't long after our first conversation that he made plans to come visit me. I remember trying to figure out what to wear. I settled on a tan sundress with flowers. He pulled up in a compact, red automatic shift car. The air conditioner didn't even work in it. We talked and enjoyed each other's company in the den of my home. Although I was raised in the church, I had recently given my life completely to Jesus Christ in January. Our mutual love for God and church was the common thread in our conversation. I was impressed with the information that he shared about our faith. I thought to myself*: he sure knows a lot about the Bible.* Later on that night, he even went to his car and shared with me some Bible study tools that he used for research. At the end of our pleasant time together, I knew that this could be going somewhere.

He was a college student that was striving to get a degree. I was about to join him on the trek to a degree as I was approaching my freshman year of college. Before starting the fall semester at his university and me my freshman year at another university, he brought his little girl over for me to meet her. I walked into the yard and greeted this precious little girl. She was so cute! I picked her up and hugged her, and she reciprocated my hug with a hug. I instantly fell in love!

Although our universities were hours away from each other, we maintained our constant contact. We must've had each other's dorm room telephone numbers on speed dial because we talked all the time. Most weekends, he came home as to be closer to me so that we could spend quality time together. We went to church together. We spent time with his daughter together. We were head over heels in love. Our relationship blossomed.

Our seemingly perfect courtship hit a few bumps in the road. I was unfaithful and admitted to him that I had been. Later, I discovered that he had been unfaithful on more than one occasion. I charged it to the fact that we were both young. I viewed it as growing pains. It was just obstacles to overcome.

On a beautiful Sunday morning in 2003, he proposed to me at church. My Pastor, Pastor's wife, and a close friend of mine were a part of the planning and execution of his proposal plan. It was such a sweet gesture because at this point we were both serving at the same church. It was such a joyous moment to share with our church family.

It was now time to plan a wedding. My Mother and I spent many Saturdays traveling to various wedding boutiques in the area to find the perfect wedding gown. I knew that I wanted a princess-cut neckline with bell sleeves. Purple is my favorite color so of course my bridesmaids would be wearing that royal color. I was preparing to marry my king.

At the same place of the engagement, is where our wedding was hosted. Our amazing church family pitched in and helped out wherever they could. When my Mother and I pulled up in the limo, I was greeted by my mother-in-law to be. She was happy. Both of our families were so happy for us. My bridesmaids looked magnificent, and they made me feel like a princess. They all told me how gorgeous I was looking, and I felt joy down to my inner core. Finally, the day that we longed for had come. The days of both of us feeling extreme sadness when having to depart was over. Now, we would be together forever. That was our plan. We made it through some tough times, and we were certain that this day was the first day of an amazing life united as one. Our wedding recessional song was Donald Lawrence's song "The Best is Yet to Come"...

Verse:
Hold on my brother don't give up
Hold on my sister just look up
There is a master plan in store for you if you just make it through
God's gonna really blow your mind
He's gonna make it worth your time
For all of the trouble you've been through, the blessings doubled just for you

Chorus:
The best is yet to come
The best, the best is yet to come

Special Chorus:
Today is the first day of the best days of your life
Today is the first day of the best days of your life

Vamp:
You ain't seen nothing, you ain't seen nothing yet

Unbeknownst to the both of us, there were some very dark days ahead. I knew that marriage came with difficulty, but I never in a million years thought that we would end up divorced. As I share some of the struggles, know that it is to both share my story and give inspiration. The purpose is to show how God gets the glory even out of ugly situations.

My ex-husband is an awesome Man of God. He has a heart of gold. He will help anybody that he can. His ability to love the unlovable has inspired me. He has a deep revelation of God's Word and has helped to teach me so much of what I know about the Christian faith. As I let you into some of what destroyed our marriage, please keep in the forefront of your mind that he is not the same man. He has sought counseling and mentorship that has restored him to the faith stronger than ever. He is actually a dear friend of mine, and I will never intentionally harm or defame him. I love him. I forgive him. There is so much that can be learned from our story. I never thought that I could have suffered hurt on such a magnitude and still pray for the person that hurt me. God used the situation and my own shortcomings to mature me and push me into purpose.

Have you made mistakes? Honestly, we all have. According to Scripture, we all have fallen to sin at some time or another. This means somewhere along the way we missed the mark. Maybe you talked negative about someone or gossiped. Maybe you caused some type of confusion. Possibly, you lied to someone or hurt them. Perhaps, you had sex outside of marriage. Whatever the fault(s) may be, you have messed up. It may have not been to the magnitude as someone else, but the point is that you nor I are in a place to look down at someone unless we are helping them up. Only God can take a mess and turn it into a message!

Don't Say That

I have four really good-looking siblings by my father but was raised by my mother and maternal grandparents as the only child in the house. My parental units made sure that I had everything that I needed and most of what I wanted. I guess you can say that I was spoiled.

I was a cheerleader from the seventh through twelfth grade and was a captain the final two years. One year, I was voted Class Favorite and elected to the Homecoming Court my sophomore through senior years of high school. I was Senior Class President. I graduated with honors from high school and with my associate degree. Everything was working out for me. I was successful at mostly everything that I had done, and I just knew that this marriage thing would be no different.

I was in no way, shape, form, or fashion the perfect wife. I married at the tender age of 22 and still had so much to learn about marriage and life in general. I would get angry with my husband when he didn't see things my way. I felt like my point of view was correct. I couldn't for the life of me understand why he didn't conform to my perspective. With disgust, I would make statements like "That is dumb," or "You are acting so stupid right now."

Sticks and stones may break my bones, but words will never hurt me. Along with Santa Claus and the Easter Bunny, this is one of the fallacies that we were led to believe as children. Words have power. It wasn't until later that I recognized how damaging my words were to him and our relationship. In a rage, I would say some mean things to him. Anger is not an excuse to be hurtful. The "I just said that because I was mad" routine will eventually get old.

Words are like seeds. If you plant apple seeds, you get an apple tree. If you plant avocado seeds, then avocados will be produced. The apple tree and avocados don't sprout immediately but eventually, will come forth. Be cautious and aware of how you speak to those that you are in a relationship with. In time, the words that you've sown into the relationship will begin to bud.

In addition to being particular with the words you choose, also be aware of the tone that you use. My ex-husband would say 'I'm not your child' and 'Don't talk to me like that.' Sometimes it's not what you say, but how you say it.

Use wisdom. A sentence sprinkled with sarcasm will not contribute to resolving a conflict. Having a discussion with "winning" in mind will cause you to lose in the end. Not laying aside pride to apologize or to ask "how can we fix this" will lead to relationship suicide.

Whether it's a spouse, friend, coworker, family member, business partner, employee, or church member, be sure to deal with conflict from a place of love and with the goal of resolution. There would be an exponential amount of arguments solved peaceably if we chose to handle them with kindness.

The Bible speaks of this area a great deal. Let's chew on these scriptures…

- Kind words are like honey—sweet to the soul and healthy for the body. Proverbs 16:24 NLT
- A gentle answer deflects anger, but harsh words make tempers flare. Proverbs 15:1 NLT
- Your words have supported those who were falling; you encouraged those with shaky knees. Job 4:4 NLT

- A word fitly spoken is like apples of gold in settings of silver. Proverbs 25:11 NKJV
- Everyone enjoys a fitting reply; it is wonderful to say the right thing at the right time! Proverbs 15:23 NLT
- The words of the reckless pierce like swords, but the tongue of the wise brings healing. Proverbs 12:18 NIV
- Let no corrupt communication proceed out of your mouth, but that which is good to the use of edifying, that it may minister grace unto the hearers. Ephesians 4:29 KJV
- Let your speech be always with grace, seasoned with salt, that ye may know how ye ought to answer every man. Colossians 4:6 KJV
- A fool's mouth is his destruction, and his lips are the snare of his soul. Proverbs 18:7 KJV
- May the words of my mouth and the meditation of my heart be pleasing to you, O Lord, my Rock, and my Redeemer. Psalm 19:14 NLT

The Ideal Couple

We were a young ministry couple that loved God and each other. He was in Seminary pursuing his Master's degree. I was working as a Respiratory Therapist, and he was working as a college ministry intern. In addition to school and his paid internship, he always kept a part-time job. Once as a security guard and another time as a valet driver. He was a hard worker. We didn't have a lot of money, but we had a lot of love.

We lived on the third floor of the college ministry building, and our rent was only $100/month. Our 3 bedroom 2 bathroom apartment was old and needed renovations. It certainly wasn't what I was familiar with, but I was willing to be wherever he was. I went in and cleaned the place from top to bottom. I painted the walls and hung borders for added elegance. My Godmother, the late Helen McGill, helped us to purchase furniture. He was living there before we got married, but now the place had a woman's touch. The entire place was wood floors, and it was quite a task to clean the floors. Yet, I took pleasure in sweeping and mopping them because this was our little spot. I was always cleaning.

My cooking needed help! To this day, I still don't eat the frozen waffles that you can pop in the toaster because we ate them so much. We had them for breakfast, as a snack, and sometimes for dinner. I fried chicken one time, and when it was bitten into, blood oozed out. He didn't complain. Later I mastered the art of frying chicken, and he said, "Baby, the first time you fried chicken, I thought it was going to get up off the plate and start walking." We laughed hysterically. I learned how to make shrimp alfredo, and that dish was a staple in our home. I also mastered hamburger helper. Needless to say, we ate out a lot.

Purpose Revealed — Jessica Smith

We were roughing it. We didn't own a kitchen table, so we used the ironing board. It served dual purposes. One day we heard something, and I brought it to his attention. He downplayed it because he knew what it was. It was a rat! Upon receipt of this information, I was ready to pack us up and move us out. I told him that the rat and I could not live in the same place. He calmed me down and assured me that he would handle it. He had traps everywhere. I later learned that it wasn't just a rat, but rats---with an s. I was grateful to have never seen them, but I knew they had been there. I was utterly disgusted. I was always cleaning, and this problem was contradictory to the atmosphere that I was creating in our little home. My Superman went to work and cleared up the problem so I could live in peace.

We were starting to get pretty good at this marriage thing. One night when he got home, he arrived to a cooked meal, me in lingerie, and the TVs in the house on ESPN (his favorite channel). I was catering to him for his hard work. He was pursuing another degree, establishing a college ministry, and working a part-time job. He was always so loving to me. I was a country girl and didn't know my way around the city, so he took me almost everywhere until I learned. New Orleans was different than my little hometown in Mississippi, and he always attempted to make me feel safe. We enjoyed spending time together and of course ministry was our priority. We were best friends. We would have arguments and disagreements, but we didn't stay mad too long.

On the outside looking in we were the perfect couple. Everything was going well for us. However, there were issues that started to present themselves. After marriage, I discovered that my husband was struggling with smoking and hid that from me. I understood that it was a problem and could be the gateway to other problems. There was no need to hide it from his support and prayer partner. We could've tackled the problem together. He tried to hide it because he didn't want to let it go. Also, the friends that he chose to hang with in New Orleans were different than the ones he had previously. I knew their names, but they never came around. I sensed, which was correct, that they were not good influences. In addition to the smoking and bad company, I caught him in some lies.

At this point, I knew there were some concerns and problems that were deeper than I knew. I prayed and trusted God that it would all work itself out in time. I told no one. This was our personal business for us to handle with each other. Plus, I didn't want to make him look bad by sharing this information. He was a minister, and I had to help maintain his reputation.

There are many couples that are in trouble. The enemy hates the institution of marriage and is out to destroy it. There are laws being established to redefine God's original definition of marriage. Marriage rates are lower than ever due to people choosing to cohabitate with no legal binding to each other.

To many, my ex-husband and I appeared to be the ideal couple. We were in trouble, and nobody knew it. Because it looked as if we had everything together, most were devastated when news of our divorce was released after eight years of marriage and 12 years together. If we would've invited a few trusted people into our private space from the beginning, then maybe it could've changed our downward spiral.

One of the greatest movies that I have ever seen is War Room. It's a story of a married couple whose relationship is in turmoil. They appeared to have the perfect life with a beautiful daughter. The husband is emotionally unattached and appears to be prideful. He considers cheating on his wife. The wife meets an older lady named Miss Clara that teaches her to fight from her knees. The "War Room" is a closet where petitions are placed on the wall, and prayer is sent up to God. At the end of the movie, the husband loses his job, and it brings him to the realization of how his actions were affecting his wife and child. Through the power of prayer, their marriage was restored.

Let's pray for marriages like never before. I admonish you to pray with fervor and intensity for your marriage (if you are married) and for other's marriages as well. Even if a relationship seems to be perfect, they still need prayer because it may not be what it looks like from the outside. If your marriage is in disarray, go into your War Room and confess the Word over it. Speak peace to confusion and harmony to disorder.

One of the most popular books on prayer is Germaine Copeland's "Prayers that Avail Much." It is full of prayers for various topics. Listed below are some prayers from the book in reference to marriage. Now, let us pray...

Peace in a Troubled Marriage

Father, in the name of Jesus, we bring _____ before You. We pray and confess Your Word over them, and as we do, we use our faith, believing that Your Word will come to pass.

Therefore, we pray and confess that _____ will let all bitterness, indignation, wrath, passion, rage, bad temper, resentment, brawling, clamor, contention, slander, abuse, evil speaking or blasphemous language be banished from them; also, all malice, spite, ill will or baseness of any kind. We pray that _____ have become useful and helpful and kind to each other, tenderhearted, compassionate, understanding, loving-hearted, forgiving one another readily and freely as You Father, in Christ, forgave them.

Therefore, _____ will be imitators of You, God. They will copy You and follow Your example as well-beloved children imitate their father. _____ will walk in love, esteeming and delighting in one another as Christ loved them and gave Himself up for them, a slain offering and sacrifice to You, God so that it became a sweet fragrance.

Satan, we render you helpless in your activities in the lives of_____ . We come against the spirit of separation and divorce, and we lose you from your assignment against them. Satan, your power is broken from their marriage in the name of Jesus.

Father, we thank you that _____ will be constantly renewed in the spirit of their minds, having a fresh mental and spiritual attitude. They have put on the new nature and are created in God's image in true righteousness and holiness. They have come to their senses and escaped out of the snare of the devil who has held them captive and henceforth will do Your will, which is that they love one another with the God-kind of love, united in total peace and harmony and happiness.

Thank You for the answer, Lord. We know it is done now in the name of Jesus. Amen.

Husbands

Father, in the beginning, You provided a partner for man. Now I have found a wife to be my partner, and I have obtained favor from the Lord. I will not let mercy and truth forsake me. I bind them around my neck and write them on the tablet of my heart, and so I find favor and high esteem in the sight of God and man.

In the name of Jesus, I purpose to provide leadership to my wife the way Christ does to His Church, not by domineering, but by cherishing. I will go all out in my love for her, exactly as Christ did for the Church — a love marked by giving, not getting. We are the Body of Christ, and when I love my wife, I love myself.

It is my desire to give my wife what is due her, and I purpose to share my personal rights with her. Father, I am neither anxious nor intimidated, but I am a good husband to my wife. I honor her and delight in her. In the new life of God's grace, we are equals. I purpose to treat my wife as an equal so that our prayers will be answered.

Lord, I delight greatly in Your commandments, and my descendants will be mighty on earth, and the generation of the upright will be blessed. Wealth and riches will be in our house, and my righteousness will endure forever. In the name of Jesus, amen.

Wives

In the name of Jesus, I cultivate inner beauty, the gentle, gracious kind that God delights in. I choose to be a good, loyal wife to my husband and address him with respect. I will not be overanxious and intimidated. I purpose to be, by God's grace, agreeable, sympathetic, loving, compassionate, and humble. I will be a blessing and also receive blessings.

By the grace of God, I yield to the constant ministry of transformation by the Holy Spirit. I am being transformed into a gracious woman who retains honor, and a virtuous woman who is a crown to my husband. I purpose to walk wisely that I may build my house. Houses and riches are the inheritance of fathers: and a prudent wife is from the Lord. In Christ, I have redemption through His blood, the forgiveness of sins, according to the riches of His grace which He made to abound toward me in all wisdom and prudence.

Holy Spirit, I ask You to help me understand and support my husband in ways that show my support for Christ. *Teach me to function so that I preserve my own *personality while responding to his desires. We are one flesh, and I realize that this unity of persons that preserves individuality is a mystery, but that is how it is when we are united to Christ. So I will keep on loving my husband and let the miracle keep happening!*

Just as my husband gives me what is due me, I seek to be fair to my husband. I share my rights with my husband.

Strength and dignity are my clothing, and my position in my household is strong. My family is in readiness for the future. The bread of idleness (gossip, discontent, and self-pity) I will not eat. I choose to conduct the affairs of my household wisely, realizing that wisdom from above is pure, peaceable, gentle, willing to yield, full of mercy and good fruits, without partiality and without hypocrisy. Amen.

The Cover-Up

I should've told. I thought that I was protecting my then husband's reputation, but was unknowingly assisting in keeping his sins in the darkness. There were lies, smoking, infidelity, and more that I was determined to pray him through. He never abused me verbally or physically. Others observed how loving he was with me. I didn't realize it then, but it was a different form of abuse. One of the seven principles of purpose by the late Dr. Myles

Munroe states that when purpose is not known that abuse is inevitable. If I take a remote control and use it as a hammer, I'm abusing it, and it gets damaged because it's being used the wrong way. That's what was happening in my marriage, and I didn't know it. My faithfulness was taken for granted. He later told me that he thought that I'd never leave. My loyalty to him and our marriage was used so that he could continue to do what he wanted. My personality is strong, so I would "pop off" when something drastic would happen with much force, but in a few days, I would get over it. He would cry, apologize, and ask to pray together and I would oblige.

With the right condition, mold and mildew can grow. Sin is the same way. Being surrounded by people that condone wrong will make you feel right about it. I learned that accountability is vital to the success of a Believer. Surround yourself with people that love you enough to tell you no when you want to hear a yes. Allow someone who cares to rebuke and correct wrongdoing and wrong-thinking. Seek to have an individual(s) in your corner that will be confidential yet confrontational with your erroneous behavior. Proverbs 15:22 states, "Without counsel purposes are disappointed: but in the multitude of counselors they are established." When I read this scripture, I said, "Wow." It was a reminder to me that wise counsel is imperative to purpose. Receiving bad advice has the ability to cause purpose to be delivered prematurely or aborted altogether.

    Darkness is a breeding ground for sin. I kept covering it up and providing the darkness that his shortcomings needed to sprout. We had access to people that I could've talked to early on to get him the help that he needed. I'm not blaming myself for his decisions, but post evaluation leads me to take my responsibility for the marriage failure. Possibly, you are hurting someone more than you are helping them. Don't assist someone in their destruction. Eventually, their private failures will result in a public fall.

    Often times in ministry, ministers are viewed as strong and having it all together. The struggles and pressure associated with ministry can be overwhelming. If not careful, being in the "limelight" can lead to pride. Occasionally ministers are still fighting demons from their past while attempting to help others overcome. This is even more of a reason that accountability is key to maintaining integrity and an upright character. Talk to someone. Seek wise counsel. You don't have to fight this fight alone.

Chapter 4: He Knows What He's Doing

In June 2005, my then husband and I moved to Montgomery, AL. We relocated from New Orleans because he received a full-time job in collegiate ministry. This was an exciting time! We joined a marvelous church and connected to some amazing people. This period in my life was pivotal to my view of church. Being a member of a progressive church that operated in excellence exposed me to a different paradigm on how to operate ministry.

Prior to connecting with the church, it was just him and me. We would ride through just to view the historic city of Montgomery. We were struggling financially and felt like his new job was the answer to our woes. His car was out of commission, and we were down to one vehicle. Early one morning, we looked outside and saw our one car being taken away. It was being repossessed! I'll never forget the feeling of helplessness. We were now in a really nice apartment, and I felt like we were about to get back on our feet. At that moment of watching them pull away, I felt so defeated.

We rented a car to get around until we could figure out how to get the car back. Right after the repossession, a broadcast of Bishop T.D. Jakes came on television. He was sharing with the congregation about his car being repossessed and how he felt at that time that he would never be able to own a car again. I was in the position that he was talking about. I related to the feelings of which he expressed. I recognized that God was speaking to me. I felt a sense of hope. As Bishop Jakes preached, it seemed as if he was invigorating my faith. We were able to get the car back in a few days and kept it until it was paid off.

Shortly after the repossession, we hit another financial bump in the road. The checking account was over $700 in the negative. I vividly recall being in church on the second row in the middle section. Praise and worship were going forth. I had a reason to be down, but instead, I chose to give God the best praise that I could. I learned how to trust God in my giving when I had little and to give Him my praise when I didn't feel it.

I had grown weary of being broke and always trying to catch up. I just knew that when we hit Montgomery soil that we had stepped into financial freedom. That was certainly not the case. It was all worked out in my head. I was working as a Respiratory Therapist and him as a College Pastor so certainly our money issues were over. I had it all figured out. Well, maybe not.

It's Going to Happen, But Not How You Think

Allow me to analyze and extract meaning from II Kings chapter 5 that will be beneficial. The passage of scripture tells of Naaman. He was the captain of the Syrian army and considered a war hero. He was valiant, courageous, and had favor with the King.

Naaman was a respected man, but he had an issue. He was a leper. During this time, leprosy was a disease that deemed one as an outcast. You can have so much going for yourself and have an issue that seems to override everything else. You can be successful and have a dilemma that is overwhelming. I encourage you not to let that area have precedence in your life. Though it is ever before you, shift your mindset and focus.

Leprosy was a disease of the skin that was visible. It's very taxing to deal with struggles that others know about. As I eventually faced a public divorce in ministry, I knew that there was much talk and many questions. To most people, even those close to us, we seemed to be the perfect couple. I had to hear about my relationship with God being questioned because my marriage fell apart. Until the writing of this book, I didn't disclose too many about the infidelity or lies. Onlookers were trying to analyze my private life for their own understanding. It was painful to realize that some even found amusement in our pain being made public.

Leprosy was also considered contagious. This is why those infected by it were quarantined. It's a disease that affected others. What a burden to bear when your misfortune, mistake, mishap, or error affects those that you care about and love. The guilt is sometimes unbearable. There's a saying that says there's no need in crying over spilled milk. This means no matter what has happened that you don't possess the ability to change history. No one can jump into a time machine, go back to a period of time, and alter actions. We can't change history, but we can certainly shape destiny.

There was a servant girl in Naaman's house that was from Israel. She stated that if her master Naaman could get to the Prophet Elisha that God would heal him of leprosy. She may have been a young girl, but she was speaking great faith.

Revelation Moment: God will speak to you through an unlikely source---When I was a Banker for Chase Bank, there was an older customer that was nice, but I didn't care to engage in an extended conversation with. He was a devout Republican and made his distaste for President Barak Obama well known. I felt that his disdain for President Obama was based in racial prejudice. One day I was walking through the lobby, and he stopped me. Internally, I was thinking "Here we go again." I was having a bad day and didn't want any part of what he was about to say. He started to tell me about him giving his life to Christ and shared how he was baptized in a creek. He shared with me how he attended the very first New Orleans Saints game. He also shared with me how there was a black man that needed help getting food, so he gave him $120 to purchase groceries. He then went on to testify how in the same day that he helped the man that he made $2,700 in the stock market. He said, "You can't beat God giving." I knew it was God speaking to me. I abruptly closed out the conversation and walked away because tears began to come to my eyes.

Out of all the people God could've used to get a Word from Him to me, he used someone that I really didn't want to talk to. He showed me the man's heart was not what I thought. A few years later, I ran into him at the local gym and shared this story with him. I let him know that he encouraged me on a day that I was feeling low. Be careful how you treat people because you may miss out on something spectacular that comes packaged in a way that you didn't expect. Say this out loud, "I'M LISTENING LORD!"

At this point in the story, Naaman has received instructions from an unlikely source. He goes to the king and tells him what the little girl said. The king sends him to the King of Israel, and he gets upset because he perceives the situation as an attempt to go to war again because of his inability to heal Naaman. Prophet Elisha hears about the situation and says send him to me. Let's read the passage below to see what happens…

Purpose Revealed　　　　　　　　　　　　　　　　Jessica Smith

9 So Naaman went with his horses and chariots and waited at the door of Elisha's house. 10 But Elisha sent a messenger out to him with this message: "Go and wash yourself seven times in the Jordan River. Then your skin will be restored, and you will be healed of your leprosy." 11 But Naaman became angry and stalked away. "I thought he would certainly come out to meet me!" he said. "I expected him to wave his hand over the leprosy and call on the name of the Lord his God and heal me! 12 Aren't the rivers of Damascus, the Abana and the Pharpar, better than any of the rivers of Israel? Why shouldn't I wash in them and be healed?" So Naaman turned and went away in a rage. 13 But his officers tried to reason with him and said, "Sir, if the prophet had told you to do something very difficult, wouldn't you have done it? So you should certainly obey him when he says simply, 'Go and wash and be cured!'" 14 So Naaman went down to the Jordan River and dipped himself seven times, as the man of God had instructed him. And his skin became as healthy as the skin of a young child, and he was healed! II King 5:914 NLT

Revelation moment: Don't be alarmed by unusual instructions—Naaman had it all figured out how things were supposed to go. He thought Prophet Elisha was going to come out to him and wave his hand. He thought that he would stand before him and make some sort of declaration to God on his behalf. Naaman was furious. He may have even felt disrespected because he made a journey and the Prophet didn't even come out to greet him. When things don't go according to plan, don't be discouraged to the point that you don't follow instructions. Divine instructions often seem unconventional. It may not make sense, but it will make miracles! As you ask God for guidance, obey His directives. If He speaks to you through a person, obey His leading. Whether you understand it or not, just obey God!

Don't give up in the midst of the process. Walking through the difficulty of confusion, aggravation, and frustration is not easy. In honesty, there were times in my journey that for a brief moment I entertained the thought of quitting. It was through prayer, praise, and faith that I was able to press through and come out of every trial stronger. The process may not feel good, but in the end, it works for your good.

My grandmother bakes the best pound cake that you will ever put in your mouth. When taking the first bite, you have to close your eyes and savor the moment. The taste buds are so pleased with her cake that I believe that if they could talk, they would express their gratitude. I've watched her many days prepare cakes for various occasions. She sifts the flour in preparation. She places the eggs, butter, sugar, and extract into the mixer. She mixes it until the consistency is right and ready to be placed into the bundt

Purpose Revealed — Jessica Smith

pan. All of the ingredients that she uses are in the cake batter, but it's not ready to eat. It must go into the heat before the process is complete. The cake batter is transformed into a delicious dessert after it endures its time in the oven. If grandmother only left the cake in the oven for 20 minutes, it wouldn't be the famous pound cake that she's known for preparing. It has to stay in the oven for a while to become what it's intended to be.

Revelation moment: The more difficult the process, the more profound the blessing—in the account of Naaman, he expressed his discontentment with the instructions to dip in the Jordan River. It was a river that was dirty. There were cleaner rivers that he could've gone to, but the Prophet sent him to the Jordan. First, things didn't go as he foresaw them. Secondly, he's received unusual directives to dip seven times. Now, he has to go to a murky place and subject himself to its filth. After laying aside his disappointment and pride, he follows the instructions that he's received. The process was full of displeasure, yet he did as he was told. What were the results? He was healed!

As you take a reflective look at your own life, I'm sure that there are instances that can be recalled that didn't work out in the way that you anticipated. Possibly, you can attest that there are some relationships that fell apart that you thought would last a lifetime. There are jobs that you planned on retiring from that you are no longer at. There are organizations that you once affiliated with that you have disconnected from. Let me assure you that things that you've been believing God for shall come to pass. You may have to go through the fire, but it is being used to make you stronger. It's going to happen, but not how you think!

Ministry is Booming

After a year of living in Montgomery, the opportunity came for my then husband to accept a full-time college ministry position with the Louisiana Baptist Convention (LBC). He was excited, but I was a bit hesitant. I was not enthusiastic about moving to that area. They brought us in and interviewed us as a couple. They also sent for us to view the campus and area. This was when excitement kicked in for me. After touring Grambling State University, I felt convinced that our team approach to ministry would be impactful. We began to make preparation to accept this new assignment and to be a blessing to the campus and community.

While there to view the area and the campus, we began to search for housing. I went into research mode. While out riding, we came across some homes that were being built. We stopped and looked at a particular home, and the contractor/owner was there. The house was not yet finished, but my husband and I were filled with hope. I went online to a mortgage loan provider and was approved for a home loan. The process to buy a home had begun. There was paperwork to gather and to submit. We went from struggling financially to now being positioned to buy our own home. I mailed the contractor a check for $500 to secure the contract. It was all a go! The loan was approved, and the contract was secure. We made a special trip back to the home again. We were in our 20s purchasing our first home. My husband gave me the liberty to do whatever I wanted to do with the home. We went to Lowe's and had a blast! I picked out the wall paint colors for each room. We picked out the light fixtures and the ceiling fans. We also were able to pick the flooring and carpet. It was such a joyous time for the both of us.

On moving day we left Montgomery, Alabama and drove to our new place of residence in Ruston, Louisiana. We unloaded and unpacked all of our belongings and placed them into our new home. At the end of the day, we were so tired. On the first night, we slept on just the mattress because we hadn't put up the beds yet. We hadn't even purchased blinds so you could see straight into the home. We did not care. We were glad to partake in this new transition together. Our marriage was doing great, and we were best friends.

We moved there in June, and my ex-husband immediately hit the campus and started grinding. He started networking and making connections. We were to establish a college ministry (Baptist Collegiate Ministry), and he was focused on the task at hand. His outgoing and humble personality was and still is liked by all that meet him. He would go into the various offices on campus and introduce himself and accept prayer requests. He became affectionately known as "Rev." At the very first worship service, there were approximately 50-60 in attendance. What a great start! I was overseeing the music ministry and working administratively.

Right before our eyes the ministry began to flourish. Every week students were piling into Grambling Hall for worship service. It was a phenomenal blessing to see these young people give their lives to Christ. Some rededicated their lives to Him. Witnessing this miracle over and over again never grew old. Praise, worship, salvation and rededication were central messages in our ministry. Seeing young people at the altar crying out to God is still amongst my fondest memories in life. They were from different states, various backgrounds, and even foreign countries, but the love that Christ gives drew us all together on one accord. The Lord used us to usher in a true revival!

The Praise & Worship team was extraordinary, and we attracted the best of the best musicians. Worship was always upbeat, energetic, and intimate. We also were honored to have the greatest leaders on the campus

Purpose Revealed — Jessica Smith

involved in the management of the ministry. As I reflect back on the Leadership Team members throughout the years, I'm delighted to have been instrumental in molding them into servant leaders. To this day, most of them are still making an impact in whatever part of the world they live in.

I started meeting with the ladies at a meeting that we called Daughters of the King. We would come together and discuss topics that were relevant to us as women. This setting allowed us to tell our personal stories and develop relationships with each other. One lady that graduated and began to work at the University was very involved in the ministry. She shared about her young son being beaten to death. Tears rolled down my face because I couldn't imagine the pain connected to her loss. I admired her strength to keep pushing after someone took her child's life. Hearing her story of loss sparked something within me. I knew that ministering to women was a part of my purpose. Her pain helped reveal to me a destiny of helping hurting women. I'm called to create atmospheres of transparency and healing. Her misfortune is not in vain. For every woman that I'm used to mentor or aid in purpose, discovery is traced back to the moment that she openly told her story. Each lady that receives a breakthrough via the ministry that God has entrusted to me can be partially accredited to another woman's hurt.

I vividly recall teaching a lesson entitled "How to Choose the Right Mate" at one of the Daughters of the King meetings. I shared with the girls how "Rev" and I met. My teaching included telling them to be cautious and careful when choosing your life partner. I typed up a sheet on pink paper with questions to ask during the dating process. I handed it out to each of them, and some of them still have it. Here it is...

Questions to Ask Before Marriage

The following set of questions is meant to spark in-depth conversations between you and a marriage prospect. These questions are just the basics. You should have long, intimate conversations about marriage before deciding to get married. Remember to look deep before you leap!

<u>Spirituality</u>
1. Are you a born again believer in Jesus Christ?
2. What do you think about the Bible?
3. After marriage, what church would we attend?
4. What church/denomination would we raise our children in?
5. Do you work or plan to actively work in the church/ministry?
6. Would you ever have a problem with me being away from home to work in the church/ministry?

7. What are your beliefs on home Bible Study/prayer?
8. What does the Bible say about marriage?
9. What does the Bible say about divorce?
10. Let's do a comprehensive Biblical study together on marriage and family.

Finances

1. Do you believe in tithing?
2. Who will be responsible for managing household finances?
3. Who will be responsible for paying the bills?
4. Discuss retirement, 401K/403B, health insurance, life insurance, stocks, bonds, etc.
5. How will we educate ourselves on financial issues?
6. How much will be put into the savings account each month?
7. Will all money be in a joint checking account or separate accounts?
8. Are both of us expected to work?
9. How will we prioritize bills?
10. Do you believe that we should discuss all or some purchases? At what dollar amount should we discuss before making a purchase?

Family

1. Who do you consider as the head of the household or the final decision maker?

2. How many children do you want? What form of discipline would you use? What type of positive affirmation would be used?

3. Will the Mother stay home and raise kids or work and put them in daycare?

4. Whose responsibility will it be to cook? How many times a week?

5. Whose responsibility will it be to clean? How should the house be kept? Will we work together to keep the house clean?

6. Feelings about in-laws—this should be a full discussion.

7. Where will we spend holidays?

8. If there are stepchildren, discuss child support, visitation, discipline, etc.

9. What are your thoughts about marriage and family counseling?

10. How will we handle arguments and major disagreements?

Sexuality

1. What does the Bible say about sex?
2. Do you believe in fidelity? Why?

3. What type of sex drive do you think you have?
4. After marriage, how often do you expect to have sex?
5. Is there a difference between having sex and making love?
6. What is romance?
7. How will we implement romance into our marriage?
8. How will we handle it if one spouse wants to have sex, and the other one is tired?
9. Have you ever had an HIV/AIDS test? Would you be willing to take one together?
10. Are there any other issues that we need to discuss?
11. Anything you need to tell me?

Social Issues

Discuss your thoughts and beliefs on the following issues:
1. Abortion
2. Pornography
3. Alcohol & Drugs
4. Smoking
5. HIV/AIDS/STD
6. Homosexuality
7. Adultery
8. Premarital sex

9. Voting & Politics
10. Domestic & Verbal Abuse

<u>Other Issues</u>
Discuss your thoughts and beliefs on the following issues:
1. The Wedding (big, small, budget, date, location)
2. Emotional Support
3. Communication
4. Respect
5. Friends (especially opposite sex friends)
6. Jealousy

Marriage is a major life decision that is a covenant between you, your spouse, and God. Remember always to be very, very prayerful when choosing a mate. With marriage comes ups and downs, but with God you and your spouse will be able to overcome any situation.

I'm now taking my own advice that I shared with the young women. I studied the dating process and coupled it with my marriage experience to teach them how to handle courtship with care. At that time, I never thought that I would experience singleness again, but here I am. I'm benefitting from previous research. Remember in every situation there is a lesson and a blessing. You have the ability to draw out the good of every bad circumstance. Yes, we experience human emotions of sadness and grief, but within us is the ability to allow it to make us better and not bitter.

I released a series of videos that I call #Saved&Single. These videos have been shared and seen by thousands via social media. I'm often called upon to minister to singles or at singles' events. I had no idea what I was being prepared for. Now, I'm planning events for Christian singles and plan to write a book entitled "Saved & Single."

Do I want to be single? No! Do I desire a husband? Yes! But, I decided to use my current situation to encourage others. While encouraging others, I actually found myself feeling more hopeful. Paul says in Philippians 4:1, "I am not saying this because I am in need, for I have learned to be content whatever the circumstances." Sometimes we find ourselves in not so ideal situations. You can choose to gripe and complain or to make the best of it. It's not that you should become complacent and hopeless. You have to take on the mentality that it is what it is, but it won't always be like this.

Another Negative Pregnancy Test

The ministry continued to grow. We faced problems with an administration which caused us to move to a local church not far from campus. Baptist Collegiate Ministry

(BCM) was the place to be on Tuesday nights at 8:15. We had a place for all. We had music ministry, hospitality ministry, women's ministry, men's ministry, fine arts ministry, evangelism ministry, and freshmen ministry. Each semester we hosted the Gift & Talent Night. This was a night of singing, dancing, spoken word, and rapping. There were times that chairs were put out to accommodate the crowd. A church of approximately 200 excited students caused the atmosphere to be electric. We were on the move, and there was no stopping us.

The ministry grew, but our family didn't. I wanted to have a baby so badly. I prayed and prayed. I asked the Lord for a set of twins. To be specific, I wanted a boy and a girl. I dreamed about the cutest little baby boy one night. He was in a car seat, and I was showing him to my grandmother in the dream. We had been trying with no success. We took our students to a conference in Alexandria, LA. A lady shared her testimony about facing infertility and how she was blessed with a child. I tried my best not to cry. The lights were turned down, and I dropped my head. I didn't want anyone to see me in a state of weakness. I couldn't hold back the waterworks. The band began to lead worship, and I released my disappointment in tears. One of the students that was sitting by me began to rub my back and console me. She said, "It's ok Mrs. Jess. God is going to bless you with a baby." I left that service with my faith restored that God would certainly answer my prayer.

I've always wanted to be a mother. My husband and I actually wanted four children—two boys and two girls. That's a lot of kids in our modern society, but we wanted a large family. We already had one (my stepdaughter) and wanted to give her siblings to play with when she came to spend time with us. We continued trying to conceive. I was praying, and we were faithfully doing what it took to get pregnant (wink).

I went to the doctor, and no reason was found for me not to get pregnant. My menstrual cycle was very irregular, so it was difficult monitoring the ovulation days. I was given Clomid (infertility medicine). The doctor informed me that the probability of conceiving twins was higher because of the medicine, and I was fine with that. All of my life, I wanted to be a mom. The thought of someone calling me Mommy warmed my heart. I would walk through the baby section in stores and get the warm-and-fuzzies. I thought about how I would dress my baby. I thought about family portraits. I planned how I would teach them to pray and love God.

Sometimes I didn't tell my husband that I was taking a test because I wanted to surprise him. One day, I was in the bathroom and my heart sunk after another negative pregnancy test. I cried. I was disappointed. I felt like less than a woman. I was confused. I couldn't understand why God wouldn't answer my prayer. I was working for Him and serving Him, but I felt like He had forgotten about me. I would hear of children being neglected or abused and get angry. I would hear of other people's pregnancies and be genuinely happy for them, yet wonder why it wasn't me. It was a burden that I carried with me for a while.

On one instance, there was a baby shower that I was invited to. It was a really rough day for me, and I didn't want to attend it. I was depressed and had been crying most of the day. My spiritual daughter, Nyomi, called and asked me about the baby shower, and I expressed to her that I wasn't going because I was feeling low and defeated. She said, "You know that they will be disappointed if you don't come." She kept encouraging me to get up and go. The last event I wanted to attend was a baby shower, but I knew that I should be there to show my support for their blessing. I went and in spite of my heartache, I had a pretty good time.

Infertility affected me emotionally. When I would go back to visit my hometown, everyone would ask "No babies yet?" Someone said to me once, "Do you need me to come show you what to do." As you can imagine this statement was like adding salt to an open wound. I went from walking through the baby section with hope to fighting back the tears. I felt so incomplete.

I'm now the proud mother of a number of spiritual babies. They call me Mama Jess. I didn't birth them, but they view me as a mother figure and I thank God for them often. If I was someone's biological mother, I wouldn't have time to mentor, train, and equip these that God has entrusted to me. I look at them and say "God, you know exactly what you are doing." It stuns me how much I adore my spiritual children. They love and respect me to the fullest. They receive correction and discipline from me. Their support of my ministry is why I'm ministering internationally. The Lord has used them to fill the void. I asked the Lord for a baby and instead He gave me several children to aid in molding.

Let me admonish you to trust God even when you don't understand. Things may not go according to plan. People may have walked away. You may have lost the job. Your children may seem to be living their lives contrary to their rearing. You may feel as if you should be over that relationship failure by now. You may feel as if God should've moved some obstacles out of the way for you by now. Don't you give up! His thoughts are not your thoughts, and His plan is greater than one that you could ever conjure up. He's got you. He's working it ALL out for your good!

Chapter 5: He Loves Me; He Loves Me Not

Our marriage was like a beautiful garden that weeds periodically kept popping up in. He was still sneaking and smoking. I was determined to hold on and pray him through. I managed the money but found out that he was doing pay day loans behind my back. Throughout all of the mishandling of our marriage, we still were best friends. We didn't argue a lot. On most days, we were in bliss with each other. It was only in flagrant situations that we experienced the bottom.

Sundays were my favorite day of the week. We would attend church, and either eat alone or most times dined with others. After dinner we would go home, cuddle up, and take a nap. Then we'd take a ride and get a snow-ball (snow cone) or a milkshake from a local restaurant named Griff's. Even if he was traveling for ministry he was usually home by Sunday.

Our life was full of laughter. We would have late night game parties at our home with some of the college students. Taboo was our favorite game. The hilarity from these nights left my stomach hurting. I cooked a Thanksgiving meal for those in our ministry that didn't go home for that holiday. We hosted Super Bowl and fight parties. There was constant cheerfulness that we were surrounded by. I wasn't the best cook in the world, but hungry college students will eat anything. They were my "guinea pigs." My cooking improved because I was doing it more often and learning to cook for the masses. Great company plus good food yielded many fun times at our home.

The college ministry was thriving. Everybody on campus knew "Rev" and they called me Mrs. Jess. We were like their parents away from home. During this time, we developed relationships of which some are still maintained to this day. We were often their counselor and advisor. Rev always sent the young ladies to me. Many Tuesday nights after service, I would be somewhere talking to a young lady. I dealt with it all! Breakups, abortion, suicide, rape, depression, academic major decisions, etc. were all dilemmas that these young people found themselves facing.

One night a young lady asked to speak to me, so we went to the back and she opened up. She expressed to me that she didn't want to live anymore. She felt as if her life was meaningless. Her hope was gone. In her mind, suicide would be the best choice for her. She laid her head down as I began to talk. I called her name and began to tell her that she had value. I told her, "This earth wouldn't be the same without you." I went on to share that for her to take her own life was not the solution, but would create a bigger problem. I remember telling her "I need you. Even my life wouldn't be the same without you." I prayed for her and came against the spirit of suicide and hopelessness in Jesus' Name. The witnessing of her bounce back is a memory that I'll hold close forever.

In another instance, we had a college student that was contemplating abortion. She was young and unwed and thought that pregnancy meant that her life would end. I was able to share with her that though the baby was conceived in sin that the baby was not sin. I encouraged her to keep the baby and realize that her baby was going to be a blessing. Now when I see pictures of her pretty little girl it warms my heart. The very child that she saw as a burden is now a blessing.

In the midst of all of this ministry, I was dealing with the ups and downs of my marriage. I was trying to trust, and my trust was constantly being violated. I held on to the wonderful and powerful man of God that he was and that others saw. Our problem wasn't that he was not supportive, left the cap off the toothpaste, or left the toilet seat up. It was character flaws which eventually tore us apart.

Author Tim Elmore explains the Iceberg Principle in his book for leaders entitled "Habitudes." It's amazing to me as I read his book just how accurate he is. I was at a conference when he shared this theory and it made a lasting impression on me.

"An iceberg is an interesting picture of the first rule of leadership. There's more to it than what meets the eye.

Purpose Revealed   Jessica Smith

Most of an iceberg is below the surface of the water. You probably remember the awesome story of the Titanic. (Maybe you saw the movie.) The huge and unsinkable ship received five iceberg warnings that fateful night of April 14, 1912, just before it went down. When the sixth message came in during the wee hours of the next morning—"Look out for icebergs"—the operator wired back, "Shut up! I'm busy." These were his last words over the wire before it all happened. Exactly thirty minutes later, the great vessel—the one whose captain said even God couldn't sink this ship—was sinking.

Hundreds of passengers and crew were drowned.

What was the problem? They forgot the truth about icebergs. What they saw above the water seemed to pose no threat. Unfortunately, most of an iceberg is below the waterline. They underestimated the power of the iceberg and overestimated their own strength. What an accurate description of so many leaders today."

Rev was a great preacher, loved God's people, loved his family, would help anybody, always sacrificed for the sake of others, had the best personality, a great sense of humor, and loved God! Yet, there were internal issues. His problems were below the surface, and the only person close enough to see them was me. Elmore goes on to say, "The iceberg represents your leadership. The 10% above the water is your skill. The 90% below the water is your character. It's what's below the surface that sinks the ship."

For the reader that is struggling with something that you know is wrong, let me encourage you to take the necessary steps to do what's right. Eventually, that secret sin will become public and embarrass you. Not only will it affect you, but those around you as well. As I think of great business leaders and religious figures that have fallen, it was due to intrinsic flaws that led to their demise. They may have been charismatic, but greedy. Their personality and skills were magnetic, but they lacked self-control. Defeat the demons in private before they are exposed. Be grateful for grace and mercy, but don't take it for granted. With loan payments, there is typically a grace period. If the payment is due on the 1st and there is a 10 day grace period, then you are not penalized if you pay within that time frame. With sin, you don't have a clue as to when your metaphorical "grace period" will come to an end. If I were you, I wouldn't chance it.

If you are in a relationship (business, romantic, platonic, etc.) with someone that is practicing an activity that will cause their ship to sink, talk to them. Don't approach with an abrasive or judgmental tone! Instead, make sure they know that you come in love and peace. Your warning may help save them from drowning. They may get angry with you, but have peace in knowing that you cared enough to warn them. Eventually, that individual will look back and say thank you for attempting to throw me a life preserver to save my life.

It Began to Fall Apart

We pastored the college ministry together. I was never overwhelmed with my roles as the overseer of music ministry, director of women's ministry, counselor, and all of the clerical duties that were entrusted to me. I actually loved it! I handled the administrative side of ministry and had access to pretty much everything. I typed up most of the ministry forms and documents that were needed. One night, I was in the computer room working on something. One of our college students was staying with us for a little bit and was sitting on the couch in the living room watching television. I was feeling suspicious and began to comb through his emails. Nothing jumped out at me. I continued searching through because I felt that something wasn't right. I went into the deleted email box and opened one up. As I looked at this particular email, I was devastated! There it was right before me. Proof that my husband was unfaithful. I got up and closed the door because I didn't want the student to walk into the room. I couldn't believe it! I began shaking from hurt and anger but stayed calm. I unplugged the laptop from the charger and walked through the living room into our room. I closed the door. He was in the bathroom, and I handed him the laptop to show him what I discovered. He looked away in shame. I didn't make a scene because I didn't want to alarm the student that was living there for the summer. I was so disappointed. How could he do this to me, after all I had done to be there for him? I kept his secrets. I prayed for him. I worked a full-time job and assisted in ministry. I tried to do everything right. I forgave him of lies and talking to other women before. But this time, I had evidence that he engaged in sexual activity with another woman. My heart was crushed. My self-esteem was smashed. There was no denying or lying his way out of this one.

    I got in the car and left. I called one of my friends, and she was the only person that I told. I was going to lose it if I didn't talk to someone. I didn't just cry; I was sobbing! My friend loved me so much that she was furious. To hear me cry was devastating to her. She knew that I had been dedicated and didn't deserve what I was currently dealing with.

    He cried and pleaded his case. He asked for one more chance. I wasn't hearing it. I was angry and convinced that he had taken advantage of my love for the last time. He would grab my hand and start praying. He said, "Let's pray together," and I replied with a no. Within a few my days my heart began to soften. I started to question my decision

Purpose Revealed   Jessica Smith

to end it all. Was he sincere this time? Did he mean it when he said that he'd hurt never me like that again? Should I throw away all of these years that I've invested into this marriage? He apologized like a million times. Even though my response was cold, one day he kneeled by the bed, grabbed my hand and began to pray. I started crying, and he grabbed me. I hugged him back. At that moment, I knew that I could not walk away. I felt like I still had to try. I felt like he needed me. I sensed that me leaving him would only make his situation worse. I started feeling sorry for him. Though my heart was shattered, I loved him.

Revelation Moment: While all of this turmoil was going on in my life, I kept doing ministry. I didn't allow my bad days to affect those around me. Until the divorce, most people had no idea of what we struggled with. I wish I would've reached out for help before things got bad, but I learned how to take a punch from life and keep fighting. I ministered to others while I was hurting. Others saw me in service and probably perceived my tears as worship when in actuality they were tears of pain. I gained from this experience the ability to do purpose while in misery.

What does this mean for you? Don't allow feelings to get you off focus. There may be bad blood between the parents of a child(ren) that are no longer together. Don't speak negatively about the other parent. You may feel mistreated or overlooked by your boss. Keep doing your job to the best of your ability. Someone may say something offensive and hurt your feelings. That's no reason to leave your church or ministry. Don't let your emotions cause you to get off track. Making decisions while emotional will lead you to undesirable results. Stay focused! Do what's right no matter how you feel.

Ministry Split

At the height of ministry, we planned to plant a church. I went to work planning and strategizing. I started reading books and scanning through websites. I acquired a demographic study of the area. I utilized an operations manual from our previous church as a resource. I obtained the Federal EIN number through the Internal Revenue Service and the state registration. I went to work on the mission and vision. I was excited because we had supporters in place. We didn't care that they were college students with no money. We just loved ministry.

Pause….As I look back, I now realize that I did everything for the church plant. By everything, I mean everything. All of the research, prep work, and orchestrating was done by me. I set up an interest meeting, and the turnout was great. I designed flyers and was ready to roll. But wait, why was I handling and setting up everything? He was to be the Lead Pastor. Not me. It's because it wasn't his vision. It was mine. I had within me the passion to establish a ministry that would impact the Nations. I'm now the founder of Kingdom Empowerment Ministries. It's an evangelistic ministry that God has birthed through me to travel and encourage others. At one point, I thought that all of the research and training that I engaged in was for naught. It all became beneficial to establish the work that was to come. As I think about it now, I must say "You did that Lord."

Press play... A young couple that we connected with began to assist us in ministry. We were excited to have help! We had a meeting and asked them about being our assistant pastors, and they eagerly agreed. We were four focused individuals that were enthusiastic about the church plant. The college ministry was prosperous and laid the foundation for us to build God a house on.

Our soon-to-be assistant pastors started befriending the key leaders in our ministry. They would host them at their house for parties and didn't invite us. I thought it to be weird because we were planning to be partners in ministry. I sensed that something was not right, but I tried to overlook it. Later, there came a misunderstanding and disagreement between them and us. The tension was visible. We had phone conversations and a meeting with no resolution. It was sad because the students were choosing sides without facts or knowledge of what was truly going on.

They started their own college ministry with the students that they developed relationships with within our ministry. We couldn't and didn't tell them that they couldn't participate. I used to encourage my husband when it would bother him. I said to him once, "We came to a town where we knew no one and look how God has blessed us. They had to steal members that we were training to build theirs."

From the college ministry, they started a church. The very ones that were supposed to help us build ministry were now helping them build a ministry. At this point was when I needed encouraging. Some of them pulled away from me, and it ripped my heart in two. I felt that they had turned their backs on me. I fed them, some slept at my house, I prayed for them, counseled them, etc. It was under our ministry that most of them were given the opportunity to operate in purpose with freedom.

This was a hard time for me because this was the first time in ministry that I experienced being lied about. One young lady said that I rolled my eyes at her. Another said that I bumped her and didn't say anything. I was so confused because all of that was not my character and I feared that others believed it. Because I stood for the truth with boldness, it was rumored that I was rough and unloving. One night after service, someone came to me and said, "Mrs. Jessica, I'm so glad that I got to know you for myself. You are nothing like what I heard." She was in association with the couple that we were now estranged from so apparently the lies concerning me were ringing within their fellowship. My Grandmother used to say that you can outlive a lie. In other words, keep living and eventually the truth will be seen. I didn't chase after what people said. I didn't call meetings with those that I heard were falsely accusing me. Instead, I stayed focused on the work that was before me. The Leadership Team needed to see me endure hardness as a good soldier. Those close to me that knew what was going on would benefit from me maintaining my integrity.

The disconnects were painful, yet beneficial. I learned to see those that vowed to be with me on the ministry journey and love them even though they walked away. I had to embrace forgiveness for those that I felt were underhanded and deceptive for their own gain. This situation allowed me to experience deliverance from resentment and bitterness. It also taught me to carefully evaluate motives.

No matter what has been done or you perceive to have been done to you, know that you have the ability to forgive. Though you may feel injured by another's words or actions, you can release it and let it go. Through prayer and your decision to be healed, you will find freedom from offense.

Stay tuned, because later on we will discuss forgiveness in more detail.

Again! Really?!

At this point, my ex-husband and I had overcome a lot. Lack of money, infertility, lies, infidelity, and a ministry split were now in our rearview mirror. We were young but overcame a great deal. I had moments where I felt uncertain. I remained hopeful and prayerful, though. I was certain that the worst was behind us. I felt that we were both focused, living for God, and determined to do right. His mistakes were in the past, and he wouldn't do anything to jeopardize our marriage anymore. In a leadership meeting one day, one of the leaders said, "Rev and Mrs. Jess, I thank God for you all. Until you all, I've never had a saved, Christian couple example and I want what you have." Wow! Tears filled my eyes because that is what I wanted.   It was always my goal for others to see our relationship as an example of God's love. Her words echoed what others thought about us. So many stated to me that they wanted a husband like mine. The young men said to him that they wanted a "ride or die" girl like me. They witnessed how loving he was to me and how respectful I was toward him.

I finished working a long day at the bank, and he was there to pick me up. I got into the car and greeted him as

Purpose Revealed   Jessica Smith

usual. My cell phone was dead, and I needed to call a friend back so I asked to use his phone and he obliged. I called my friend, and she didn't answer. I started scrolling through his text messages and found one that sparked concern. He had been texting some girl. I messaged her as if I were him to gain more information and this situation was not looking good. I asked him about it, and he said that he'd be honest and admit that he met a girl and was communicating with her via the phone, but that was it. Before we pulled up in the garage, I sent her a text and told her that this is his wife texting you. I let her know that I wasn't approaching her in a rude manner, but that I wanted to know what was going on with my husband. She responded, "Call me."

We walked into the house, and I sat on the couch. He walked into our room, and I grabbed the keys from the table and his phone and left. I knew he couldn't follow me because our other vehicle was broken. I drove up the street and proceeded to call the woman that he had been texting back and forth with. I introduced myself and told her that I was his wife. I reiterated the fact that I didn't have an issue with her, but deserved to know what was going on. She said, "I didn't know that he was married. He didn't tell me. We've been talking on the phone for a few months now." I asked her how they met, and she said on the internet. She dropped the bomb when she said, "I think I've been to your house." She went on to describe my bathroom to me. She said that she felt that something wasn't right because she saw a curling iron on top of a tall white cabinet. She was right! Her description was accurate. She willingly answered every question that I asked. I was in shock!

She went on to tell me exactly when she was there. It was the weekend that I went home to Mississippi for my best friend's initial sermon. I was away to support my friend's acceptance to the call of ministry, and he was spending time with another woman. She slept in my bed. She showered in my bathroom. She used the towels that I bought. She sat on the couch that we cuddled up on. She watched the flat screen TV that we recently purchased. She walked on the carpet that I chose. She slept under the fan that I picked out. My mind was racing!

After our detailed, thorough conversation, I went back home, and he was sitting on the couch. He just sat there because he knew. I said, "So I talked to your little friend," in a calm, cynical tone. I let him know that she told me *EVERYTHING*! He said, "I know I'm sorry won't fix it. You've given me chances, and I don't blame you for leaving. I don't want you to, but I don't blame you." I asked, "Did you even change my sheets?" He just sat there with a look of shame and embarrassment on his face. I didn't raise my voice or yell. I peacefully walked into the bathroom and took a shower. In the shower, I sang a song and gave God praise. He was probably confused and thought that I was losing it. That wasn't the case at all. A peace came over me that I'm yet to understand.

Once again, my trust was violated, and my heart was broken! What was wrong with me that my husband would go outside of our marriage again? I knew that I was a good wife. I prayed for others and for him too. Over the years, I gained weight so was it because of that? Was I not pretty enough? I questioned everything about myself. When I asked why he did what he did his only response was "selfish." He told me that there was nothing wrong with me and that he was the one with the problem.

This time, I was serious about no longer tolerating his mistreatment of me. No longer was I going to put my health at risk. I became angry and wanted it to be over. I needed time, and I started to plan my exit strategy. I was determined to move on and not allow my heart to be hurt by anyone ever again (so I thought…keep reading).

One of the hardest things that I've ever done was when I sat down to tell the Leadership Team that Rev and Mrs. Jess were getting a divorce. I told him to come tell them with me, but he didn't show up. They were devastated! The young men walked off together, and the girls sat there with me. They kept asking me if it was a joke. They were in disbelief! The guys took it harder than the girls. I was angry all over again because he made me do this by myself.

Let me pause here to give a reminder that my ex-husband has grown into a man that has used his mistakes and hardships to make him stronger. We talk periodically, and I'm proud of his progress. He's a reminder of God's grace and mercy. He took the time to be restored and now his testimony of freedom will bless people across the world. He's a reminder that no matter how low a person falls, that God's Hand is extended to reach down and pick you up.

Revelation moment: God's love is endless and unconditional! No matter what you've done, He still loves you. When I think about how God still loved me even though I missed the mark, I couldn't help but love even those that wounded me. Every time I sinned, I offended God. I've hurt him more times than anyone on the planet could ever hurt me. Every time I disobeyed Him, I disappointed Him and broke His heart. Yet, he forgave me and loved me. Lord, thank you for loving me! Chew on these Scriptures…

Romans 5:8 But God demonstrates his own love for us in this: While we were still sinners, Christ died for us.

Ephesians 2:4-5 But because of his great love for us, God, who is rich in mercy, made us alive with Christ even when we were dead in transgressions—it is by grace you have been saved.

Purpose Revealed   Jessica Smith

Romans 8:37-39: No, in all these things we are more than conquerors through him who loved us. ^{3}For I am convinced that neither death nor life, neither angels nor demons, neither the present nor the future, nor any powers, neither height nor depth, nor anything else in all creation, will be able to separate us from the love of God that is in Christ Jesus our Lord.

John 3:16:For God so loved the world that he gave his one and only Son, that whoever believes in him shall not perish but have eternal life.

I John 4:9-11: This is how God showed his love among us: He sent his one and only Son into the world that we might live through him. This is love: not that we loved God, but that he loved us and sent his Son as an atoning sacrifice for our sins. Dear friends, since God so loved us, we also ought to love one another.

Sometimes my husband made me feel like the most loved woman in the world. Other times I wasn't feeling the love at all. Those that declared their lifetime connection made me feel special with their encouraging words. When they walked away, I was left feeling scorned. I've had friends that made me sound like Jesus' little sister until I heard that their words were quite the contrary in my absence. People can be finicky. They may be here today and gone tomorrow. They may love you this moment and hate you the next. Allow no one's actions or words to cause you to hate them.

"Now there is a final reason I think that Jesus says, "Love your enemies." It is this: that love has within it a redemptive power. And there is a power there that eventually transforms individuals. Just keep being friendly to that person. Just keep loving them, and they can't stand it too long. Oh, they react in many ways in the beginning. They react with guilt feelings, and sometimes they'll hate you a little more at that transition period, but just keep loving them. And by the power of your love, they will break down under the load. That's love, you see. It is redemptive, and this is why Jesus says love. There's something about love that builds up and is creative. There is something about hate that tears down and is destructive. So love your enemies."

-Dr. Martin Luther King, Jr.

The love of God is constant and consistent. He is the one that you will always be able to depend on. As children, many of us played the "he loves me, he loves me not" game. It was a game of chance. There was always the possibility of ending on he loves me not. With God, there is no luck involved. He always loves you. Even if you don't feel it, He still loves you. Say this out loud, "HE LOVES ME!"

Chapter 6: I've Been Dropped

Even after the last bout of infidelity, I still had doubts. I knew that I couldn't tolerate this type of mistreatment any longer, but was still wearisome about leaving the man that I was in love with all of my adult life. I fell in love with him at 18, and I was now 30 years old. Did I want to forfeit all of those years? Was I not trusting God if I decided to end the marriage? What about the people that would be affected? How could a seemingly perfect couple that believes in God not make it last? Questions and fear filled my mind.

My ex-husband was a college ministry superstar. He traveled and met other college pastors. Conferences and meetings were sprinkled throughout his schedule. He would often share his testimony, and it blessed others. Those in the field of college ministry were astonished at his ability to plant and grow such a thriving ministry so quickly. They picked his brain about how he could go into an area that he knew no one and now have over 150 people consistently showing up for worship service. He went to meetings and received phone calls from others asking his advice about a field that they had been in longer than him. Of course, he willingly shared his experience and insight. But I believe that he left something off. He was sharing his tactics and strategies to win souls for Christ, but I knew the real answer. He was (and still is) ANOINTED!

Pause: Let me share with you information from a website (www.gotquestions.org) that I sometimes refer to for studying purposes. It's a site that poses an answer to a Biblical question.

Question: What is the anointing? What does it mean to be anointed?

Answer: The origin of anointing was from a practice of shepherds. Lice and other insects would often get into the wool of sheep, and when they got near the sheep's head, they could burrow into the sheep's ears and kill the sheep. So, ancient shepherds poured oil on the sheep's head. This made the wool slippery, making it impossible for insects to get near the sheep's ears because the insects would slide off. From this, anointing became symbolic of blessing, protection, and empowerment.

The New Testament Greek words for "anoint" are chrio, which means "to smear or rub with oil" and, by implication, "to consecrate for office or religious service"; and aleipho, which means "to anoint." In Bible times, people were anointed with oil to signify God's blessing or call on that person's life (Exodus 29:7; Exodus 40:9; 2 Kings 9:6; Ecclesiastes 9:8; James 5:14). A person was anointed for a special purpose—to be a king, to be a prophet, to be a builder, etc. There is nothing wrong with anointing a person with oil today. We just have to make sure that the purpose of anointing is in agreement with Scripture. Anointing should not be viewed as a "magic potion." The oil itself does not have any power. It is only God who can anoint a person for a specific purpose. If we use oil, it is only a symbol of what God is doing.

Another meaning of the word anointed is "chosen one." The Bible says that Jesus Christ was anointed by God with the Holy Spirit to spread the Good News and free those who have been held captive by sin (Luke 4:18-19; Acts 10:38). After Christ had left the earth, He gave us the gift of the Holy Spirit (John 14:16). Now all Christians are anointed, chosen for a specific purpose in furthering God's Kingdom (1 John 2:20). "Now He who establishes us with you in Christ and has anointed us is God, who also has sealed us and given us the Spirit in our hearts as a guarantee" (2 Corinthians 1:21-22).

Just because you are anointed doesn't mean that you aren't subject to fall. It doesn't disqualify you from mistakes. We all have witnessed the fall of someone that we deemed to be "anointed." They will pray for others to be set free and still struggling in private. In the book of I Samuel, David was anointed to be king, yet he messed up. He saw a woman named Beethsheba outside bathing one day and liked what he saw. In spite of her being married, he committed adultery with her, and she became pregnant with his child. He tried to cover it up by sending for her husband Uriah to come home from battle to lay with her. That plan didn't work so David gave orders to have him placed in the forefront of the army which caused him to die. David was powerful, yet he had problems. He was a worshipper, yet had woes. He was king, yet had kinks.

Revelation moment: I'm certainly not giving a pass to sin. I'm issuing a warning! I have learned that even on my best day that I have within my flesh the capability of falling. I'm a preacher, counselor, entrepreneur, and spiritual mother, yet I'm not exempt from the struggle to do what I know to be right. The advice that I've administered, I have to apply to my own life at times. The wickedness that I encourage others not to engage in has been a struggle for me to stay away from. I have to remind myself that it's not worth it when I desire to say or do something contrary to God's will. "What is the best thing about being in God's will," was a question that my Pastor (Maize Warren, Jr.) posed to us one night in our weekly life group. Various responses were given, but his answer still rings within me. He said, "The best thing about being in God's will is that He is there." Wow! Where He is, is where we should desire to be. Everything that we need is in Him. He possesses love, joy, peace, forgiveness, deliverance, salvation, and provision just to name a few. Sin will always lead you to operating outside of the will of God for your life. It's not worth it!

They Let Us Fall

My ex-husband was a full-time employee of the Louisiana Baptist Convention. They supported him and provided the resources that were needed to be successful in the ministry. He was featured in articles and highlighted at some of the meetings because of the productivity of the Baptist Collegiate Ministry (BCM) at Grambling State University. He was known throughout the state for the great work that he was doing. What they didn't know is that he was facing struggles that lingered from childhood. No one discerned that though he was producing great fruit that his roots needed tending.

He decided that the battle he had been facing was too big for him to continue trying to fight it alone. After the discovery of the adulterous affair that took place in our home, he reached out for help. Out of all the years of fighting, he finally sought help for the demons that he was combatting. He opened up to his boss which was the State Director of BCM. The conversation was established as being confidential at its inception. He was then put in contact with a Christian counselor that was affiliated with their association. He went to her and opened up. He exposed himself because he knew that he needed assistance to overcome. He shared with me his encounter with seeing a counselor for the first time. I saw something shift in him and felt a spark of hope.

One week later, his boss asked to meet with him and told him to bring his laptop. When he arrived at the meeting, it was his boss and another college minister. He thought that this was a follow-up meeting to monitor his progress. He fired him! Just like that, they let him go. All of the hard work and great light that was shone upon their organization apparently didn't matter. He sought help from a Christian organization, and they dropped him. He asked for aid and received punishment. He was seeking restoration and instead was issued termination.

I was away for training for my new job as a Banker. I was on lunch break, and he called me right after the meeting. I could hear the distress in his voice when I answered the phone. He told me what transpired in the meeting. I did my best to comfort and console him. He was in shock and disbelief. He shared with me that the last words that his now former boss told him was, "In this case, the devil won." What type of Christian leader would say that? What type of Believer would spew such hopelessness? What is wrong with him? These thoughts went through my mind, but I still responded in faith. I boldly declared to him, "I don't care what happens, God is still going to take care of us."

Purpose Revealed Jessica Smith

After this, I watched him struggle. His belief was shaken. His hope was lost. We relaunched the ministry independent of the LBC because I refused just to drop the students that were connected. They never sent one representative to check on the students. This caused me to doubt if they even cared about them. I thought to myself: *were we the black ministry that was used to make their predominately white denomination seem diverse?* I was practically running the ministry alone at this point, and it was very difficult. He actively searched for jobs. Every day he was on the computer and visiting businesses with job vacancies. We struggled to pay the mortgage, and it fell behind. I didn't make enough money to cover all of the bills, so we were in a financial tight.

To this day, not one person has called to ask how I was doing. Every year, all of the campus ministers and their spouses and families went to a retreat together. In my mind, we were a family and in this together. No one reached out to see how our marriage was sustaining the blow. It was a painful thought because I was under the perception that they cared about us beyond college ministry. I'm not saying that he shouldn't have been removed, but someone should've reached out and tried to restore him. In my view, the entire Louisiana Baptist Convention expressed a lack of care or concern. No one tried to refurbish our failing marriage. They dropped us!

II Samuel 9:1-11 has many revelation moments. Let's dig in…

One day David asked, "Is anyone in Saul's family still alive—anyone to whom I can show kindness for Jonathan's sake?" [2] He summoned a man named Ziba, who had been one of Saul's servants. "Are you Ziba?" the king asked. "Yes sir, I am," Ziba replied. [3] The king then asked him, "Is anyone still alive from Saul's family? If so, I want to show God's kindness to them." Ziba replied, "Yes, one of Jonathan's sons is still alive. He is crippled in both feet." [4] "Where is he?" the king asked. "In Lo-debar," Ziba told him, "at the home of Makir son of Ammiel." [5] So David sent for him and brought him from Makir's home. [6] His name was Mephibosheth; he was Jonathan's son and Saul's grandson. When he came to David, he bowed low to the ground in deep respect. David said,

"Greetings, Mephibosheth." Mephibosheth replied, "I am your servant." [7] "Don't be afraid!" David said. "I intend to show kindness to you because of my promise to your father, Jonathan. I will give you all the property that once belonged to your grandfather Saul, and you will eat here with me at the king's table!" [8] Mephibosheth bowed respectfully and exclaimed, "Who is your servant, that you should show such kindness to a dead dog like me?" [9] Then the king summoned Saul's servant Ziba and said, "I have given your master's grandson everything that belonged to

Saul and his family. [10] You and your sons and servants are to farm the land for him to produce food for your master's household. But Mephibosheth, your master's grandson, will eat here at my table." (Ziba had fifteen sons and twenty servants.) [11] Ziba replied, "Yes, my lord the king; I am your servant, and I will do all that you have commanded." And from that time on, Mephibosheth ate regularly at David's table, like one of the king's own sons.

    Mephibosheth was the son of Jonathan and the grandson of King Saul. King Saul had a disaster for David. In spite of King Saul's jealousy of David, his son Jonathan was close friends with him. Once David became king he desired to show kindness to any of Saul's relatives that were still alive because of Jonathan. Mephibosheth was the lone survivor. He had a disability that caused him not to be able to walk. In II Samuel 4, the answer is given as to how he became crippled. When news came about the death of Saul and Jonathan, Mephibosheth's nurse ran away in haste and dropped him.

    What do you do when you are dropped by the one that is supposed to take care of you? You may have been in relationships where instead of loving you, they used you. It may have been a family member that was supposed to be caring for you, but they molested you. Possibly, there was an individual that took advantage of their authority and misused you for their own selfish gain.

Mephibosheth's condition was of no fault of his own. His life was affected because of the mistake of someone else. There were days that in the midst of it all that I would be angry about the conditions that I was enduring because of the decisions of someone else. I felt as if my suffering wasn't fair. I was working in ministry, serving God, helping others, keeping my house clean, and being a good wife.

Revelation Moment: The process is birthing the promise. The Children of Israel experienced the wilderness before they possessed the Promised Land. The pit was essential so that Joseph could get to the palace. The cross was necessary for Jesus' Resurrection. In order for there to be a Resurrection, there first had to be a Crucifixion. The lyrics to a popular hymn are, "Must Jesus bear the cross alone, and all the world go free? No, there's a cross for everyone, and there's a cross for me." I now understand that my journey has been my cross. I've had sleepless nights. I've battled depression. I've been broken. Yet, I have been blessed to look back and say that the Lord has kept me. My metaphorical cross is the reason that you are reading this book. The pain pushed me into purpose!

King David sends for Mephibosheth. His family is dead, and he is the lone survivor. It was customary that a new dynasty would kill all the descendants of the prior dynasty. In sports, sometimes a newly hired head coach will clear out the staff. He hires his own staff because he wants those that are loyal to him and won't usurp authority. So can you imagine how terrified Mephibosheth must've been? David has to tell him not to be afraid because he sent for him so that he could do something nice for him.

Pause: What you thought was going to kill you, is actually going to bless you. Your misery will become your ministry. Your test will become your testimony. Your mess will become a part of your message. Your setback will become a stage. Your trial will lead to triumph. Your headache will give someone hope. Your burden will result in a blessing. Ask me how I know—because it happened for me!

King David tells Mephibosheth that he will now eat at the table with him. He went from Lodebar (meaning no pasture, no word, no communication) to the King's table. Also, all of the land that belonged to Saul, he gave to him. He is now a landowner and being treated like royalty. King David tells Saul's former servant, Ziba, that he and his servants will till the land for Mephibosheth. He was able to enjoy the benefits of ownership without the labor that typically comes with it. This is supernatural favor! His new position allowed for a new possession.

I've prayed for every reader that is reading this book. Mephibosheth experienced an expeditious turnaround, and I pray that same favor over you and your family. You may have felt thrown to the ground, but you are getting up better than ever. I call it the "basketball anointing." If you bounce a basketball lightly, it doesn't bounce that high. But if you bounce it really hard it will go high into the air. The harder you are thrown down, the higher you will bounce back.

Revelation moment: II Corinthians 4:8-9 says, "We are troubled on every side, yet not distressed; we are perplexed, but not in despair; persecuted, but not forsaken; cast down, but not destroyed." We were dropped by an organization that I thought truly cared about us. Our marriage suffered and eventually died because when they were sought after for help, they just threw us away. When I look at my ex-husband's strength and growth, I can say that his ex-boss was wrong. The enemy didn't win! As I evaluate my own life, I'm in awe that I am stronger than ever and continuing to help encourage others. I was dropped, but not destroyed!

The Power of Restoration

"Brothers, if someone is caught in a sin, you who are spiritual should restore him gently. But watch yourself, or you also may be tempted. Carry each other's burdens, and in this way, you will fulfill the law of Christ" (Galatians 6:1-2 NIV).

I planned to outline the proper steps of restoration. I intended to give tips and advice from my experience. I decided against that because my input on the subject is simplistic and to the point. Love your brother and sister enough to hold their hand and guide them back to the Cross. As I was perusing various sources about restoring the fallen sinner, I read the conclusion of the article listed below that touched my heart….

    The hymn writer I mentioned earlier, Robert Robinson, was a wild young man who lived a debauched life as a teenager. At age 17, he went with some friends to scoff at the famous Evangelist, George Whitefield. But Robinson was so impressed by Whitefield's preaching that he got saved. At 23, he wrote the hymn, "Come Thou Fount of Every Blessing." For many years, he served as a Baptist pastor, but later in life, he got involved with the doctrines of Unitarianism and strayed from the Lord.

    One day he was riding in a stagecoach when he struck up a conversation with a woman. When she realized that he was well informed on spiritual matters, she asked him what he thought of a hymn she had just been reading. To his astonishment, he found that it was the hymn, "Come Thou Fount," which he had written as a young man. He burst into tears and told her, "I'm the poor, unhappy man who wrote that hymn many years ago. I would give anything to have back the joy I knew then." The woman assured him that the "streams of mercy" referred to in the song still flowed. Robinson was deeply touched, turned his wandering heart again to the Lord, and experienced His grace and forgiveness.

That same grace is available to all who have failed the Lord. If you will turn back to Him, He will abundantly pardon and restore you to fellowship with Him and to service in His cause. You may be a great sinner, but Jesus is a greater Savior!

Chapter 7: How?!

After my ex-husband's termination and lack of support from those he sought for help, things grew even more difficult. He went away to train as a truck driver, and that was a strain on top of our tedious journey. I was holding down the ministry. We launched under the name Ignite. I refused just to drop these God-fearing students that loved ministry.

Even though worship service started at 8:00 p.m., the Leadership Team reported early. He and I walked in together, and we told them that we were going to work it out. They jumped and ran and celebrated. They hugged us and were filled with exuberance!

He wasn't around much because he was training. I was working full-time and managing the ministry practically alone. In spite of all that went on, the ministry was still blessed. We took some hits personally, financially, and relationally. We also suffered a ministry blow. I wasn't accustomed to doing ministry without him. I was used to having my partner by my side through the good and bad times.

Revelation moment: The Lord taught me to depend solely on him. He was teaching me how to trust him even in the midst of confusion. I didn't know until I was put in this position that I had within me the ability to oversee a ministry. It was on-the-job training for what was to come.

One evening, my then husband came home from truck driving school. I asked him to change the light bulbs on the outside and some more things around the house. He took out the garbage and helped out with the things that I asked him to do. He said that he was going to hang out with some men. I didn't feel comfortable with them because my discernment told me that they had the same struggles as him. Our marriage was on thin ice, and it seemed to me that he would want to stay home and work on rebuilding. While he was gone, years and years worth of anger, hurt, pain, resentment, bitterness, and disgust kicked in. I called his phone, and he didn't answer. At this moment, I drew the conclusion that his situation was worse than before and that I was done. I walked into the master bathroom. We had his and her closets. In a rage, I entered into his closet and pulled down all of his clothes that were on hangers onto the floor. I took everything off the top shelves and placed it all on the floor of the closet as well. I opened up his bathroom drawers and poured what was in them onto the pile. Everything under his side of the sink was added to the heap. Then, I walked into the bedroom and removed his underwear, shirts, and socks from the chest of drawers and threw it on top of everything else.

I now know that I suppressed my feelings. I had to be the strong one. I was the prayer warrior. I was the stable one. I ministered to him and tried to help him while I was hurting. Finally, I broke. I was like an impending volcanic eruption. I couldn't take it any longer. I wanted out!

I was asleep when he arrived back home that night. The next morning he let me know that he saw that I had thrown all of his stuff on the floor in his closet. I responded, "Yes I did, and I want you out by the time I get home from work. If not, I'll call the police." This was the beginning of the end.

After our separation, I was handling the ministry alone. Of course, everyone wondered about the whereabouts of Rev., but the last they knew is that he was away training to be a truck driver. I was never able to get the heart to tell them that we were over for good this time.

While preparing for worship service one night, I broke down. I was hauling heavy sound equipment from the house to the car. This used to be one of his weekly tasks. I was furious because I now had to do it alone. My makeup needed to be touched up after breaking a sweat. Before I knew it, tears rolled down my face, and I paused. I felt so alone. Until this moment, I always had him to fight through the difficult times. Even if it was pain caused by his decisions, he was still there. Now, I was all by myself.

Time to Move On

The time came for me to take care of me. I stopped struggling to pay the mortgage note and started saving my money to make a move. I was ready for a change. I formulated a mental list of the cities that I was considering: Atlanta, Dallas, Jacksonville, or back to Montgomery. It was a bittersweet consideration. I had grown fond of the country area that I lived in for 6 years. I met some of the greatest people ever during that time. Oh, and my students, which I viewed as my babies, were my heart. It was not easy, but I made the decision to do what was best for Jess. It was settled that I was moving to the city.

I was at work one day after returning from a funeral back home. I felt a tug to come back closer to home. I went to my company's intranet page and saw that there was an opening for my position in Slidell, LA. It was only 45 minutes from my hometown of Poplarville, MS. I applied even though being back closer to home was not a part of my plan. I interviewed, and it went well. When I arrived back to work, I was informed that the position was being offered to me. What was I going to do?

One Saturday morning I was cleaning the house and praying. I recall saying, "God, I need you to tell me what to do and make it plain. I want to be in your will, so I need you to speak to me about my next move." I went about my day and started to prepare for a concert that evening at

Louisiana Tech University. I was the MC that night, and we had a great time. A Woman of God walked up to me while I was sitting in the front row and asked if she could pray for me. I reluctantly said yes because I didn't know her. She got on her knees and laid her hands on my feet. She started out her prayer with the portion of scripture that says, "How beautiful are the feet of them that preach the gospel." She continued to pray. Then she looked at me and said, "It is the Lord that is calling you back to that area. You have what the people are hungry for. You possess the anointing that they need." I began to cry because I knew EXACTLY what she was referring to. I asked the Lord to speak, and He did.

Revelation moment: Be on the lookout for the voice of God! I didn't expect to receive my answer in that way. I also wasn't expecting Him to answer me so quickly. In the New Testament, we see Jesus performing miracles in various ways. He didn't heal the exact same way every time. The Lord is speaking to you. Are you listening? Have you turned others away that He could've sent to give you a message? Have you overlooked a sign on the road that was a memo from Heaven? He's a big God that cares about even the little aspects of your life.

When I arrived back to work that Monday morning, I sent an email to inform them that I would accept the transfer. I knew that God had given me my answer. Even though it didn't align with my plans, I knew that His will was what was best for me.

"Many are the plans in a person's heart, but it is the LORD's purpose that prevails." This situation revealed Proverbs 19:21 to me on a very relatable and intimate level. I admonish you to submit all of your plans to the Lord. Let Him lead and guide your path. There is safety and protection in His will. Even when calamity strikes, being in the right place at the right time will always lead to victory.

Pause: Let's meditate on scriptures in reference to purpose…

'The Lord will fulfill his purpose for me; your steadfast love, O Lord, endures forever. Do not forsake the work of your hands.' Psalm 138:8

'And we know that for those who love God all things work together for good, for those who are called according to his purpose.' Romans 8:28

'I cry out to God Most High, to God, who fulfills his purpose for me.' Psalm 57:2

'So, whether you eat or drink, or whatever you do, do all to the glory of God.' I Corinthians 2:31

'Or do you not know that your body is a temple of the Holy Spirit within you, whom you have from God? You are not your own, for you were bought with a price. So glorify God in your body.' I Corinthians 6:19-20

'For we are his workmanship, created in Christ Jesus for good works, which God prepared beforehand, that we should walk in them.' Ephesians 2:10

'The purposes of a person's heart are deep waters, but one who has insight draws them out.' Proverbs 20:5

'But seek first the kingdom of God and his righteousness, and all these things will be added to you.' Matthew 6:33

Press play: Then came moving day. It was a steamy summer day in June. I collected boxes for weeks and started preparing for relocation. I packed up glasses and plates. I wrapped my crystal from the wedding in newspaper. I labeled boxes with a marker. I packed my car and my Mother's car with clothes. My friends came to help me load the moving truck with my dining table, bedroom set, and living room furniture. It was great to have help. I had been dealing with the separation, and it was hard. I felt support, and that was refreshing.

I'll never forget closing the door for the last time. The house was in foreclosure. I was saying goodbye to the place that I was so proud to call home. I was bidding farewell to the memories. I was parting from the ministry that I struggled to make survive. I was leaving the marriage that I wanted to work so badly. A portion of me felt like I lost. I stood there for a minute as if to say goodbye to that season of my life. It was hard! My Mother looked and asked if I was ok. I responded yes, but my emotions were all over the place. Everything seemed to be changing around me. My friend that came to help me move said, "Let's pray."

> Closed Doors Lead To Open Doors
> By: M.S. Lowndes
> "There are times in our lives,
> We come to a closed door
> It does not always mean that we
> Have not heard from the Lord
> It may only mean that God
> Is changing how we get there,
> To show to us a better way
> That we were unaware
> So don't see this as an end
> To the outworking of God's will,
> The thing that God has birthed in you,
> He wants to see fulfilled
> Just continue to trust in Him
> And leave it in His hands,
> He will work this whole thing out,
> For it is what He has planned
> And as we look back, we will see
> How God had been our guide
> And directed us along the path
> Where doors stood open wide

> So thank Him for these hard times,
> The setbacks we go through,
> For, it is God who is leading us
> To make our dreams come true."

Revelation moment: The closed door is a blessing that will lead to greater doors! It sparks redirection in your life. You have to be tenacious in your faith and trust God even when you don't understand. It builds character. Allow it to teach you steadfastness. A closed door is an indication that new opportunities are coming from sources that are unfamiliar. New doors are opening.

Back on the Market

While going through the divorce, I faced some dark moments. I cried and was crushed. I was embarrassed. I felt low, and my self-esteem was negatively affected. I knew that people wanted to know what happened, but I didn't share with many. Sometimes, I would lay in bed and cry at night. I asked the Lord to take the pain away.

One of my uncles is a pastor. He and his wife (my mom's sister) allowed me to sit down and talk to them about the divorce. My aunt told me not to speak negatively about him because though he made mistakes that he was still a "man of God." This was some of the best advice that I received during the transition. I could've damaged him even more with my words. I would've been speaking from a place of hurt and harmed even myself. It took years for me to start talking about some of the details of the relationship. I had to go through the pain and grow through the process. I am in a place that I'm able to share the story from a pure heart. Now, the story can be told from a place of healing to administer healing. If I would've spoken on my journey too soon, I feel that I would've possibly spread bitterness like a highly infectious disease.

    I needed a healthy way to release the stress, pressure, and pain of what I was going through. I was speaking with a friend one day, and he gave me the answer. He started to talk to me and asked me why I accepted the mistreatment that I did for so long. Then, he asked if it contributed to my weight gain. He said, "You are a beautiful woman and your face has not changed, but you need to get that weight off of you." I was shocked. Yet, I knew that he was right. He went on to talk about how I was so disciplined in other areas and needed to get some restraint in the area of my physical health. This was a wake-up call. Shortly after this blunt conversation, I joined the gym.

    At the commencement of my weight loss journey, I weighed 230 pounds. I started monitoring my calories with an app on my phone. The calorie counter helped me to manage my intake, and I was giving more attention to what and how much I ate. The gym was my place of release.

The treadmill and elliptical became my friends. I would religiously be at the gym at 5:30 am. I felt a sense of pride after each workout. I was doing something for me. My weight loss was evident. My clothes started to fit differently, and even my face was appearing slimmer.

The one question that I was asked the most during the trek to a healthier me was "how." Everyone wanted to know my secret. They wanted to know what was being done to lose the weight. People would ask me on my job or send me messages asking me about how they could lose weight. My answer was always the same. I informed them that I was cutting calories and hitting the gym up to five days a week. I let the inquirers know that if I could do it that they could too.

What I didn't tell them was that I had a little extra motivation. I was back on the market! I was with the same man from the age of 18, and I was now 30 years old. A lot changed during those 12 years, and I was revamping myself. I was getting it together because I wasn't planning on being single for long. As the young people say, I was trying to get "chosen." I was chosen alright, but not how I thought.

I knew that there was the call of God on my life to preach the Gospel. I would sit in service and cry because I knew preaching was a part of my purpose but didn't want it to be. I understood that to whom much is given that much is required. I had been through enough and wasn't excited about signing up for the battles that came along with being a minister. Also, I was raised to believe that a woman was not supposed to preach. Even to this day in my hometown, a woman is not allowed to step foot in the pulpit in the majority of the churches. I've always wanted to make my family proud, and this would certainly be embarrassing to them. There were no female preachers in my family. I had no one to reference or to mentor me. The inward struggle was intense.

I was sitting in a service and once again the Lord made His answer plain to me. My Pastor was preaching in Monroe, LA. At the end of his sermon, he called me up during the altar call. He asked a visiting lady preacher to anoint my ears. Then, he asked for all of the clergy to lay hands on me and to pray. I felt the power of God and tears rolled down my face. I couldn't take it any longer. I could no longer deny it. My running came to a halt. When I got back to my seat, I pulled out my cellphone and sent a text message to my Mother and a few friends to let them know that I accepted my call to preach the Gospel. I was chosen… by God!

It's a Boy
After moving back closer to home, I was licensed to preach the Gospel. It was during this time that my personal

ministry began to soar. I was inspired to launch a worship service in my hometown. The name of it was Fresh Fire. By this point, I was blessed to have made connections that were beneficial to my life and ministry. These people saw the vision and were (and still are) extremely supportive.

We were diligently making preparation for the first Fresh Fire service at The Dixon Theatre in Poplarville. I hosted conference calls, and we passed out flyers. The service was going to be held periodically with the goal of bringing a fresh worship experience to that town. It was designed to be unique and refreshing. The praise and worship was going to be upbeat and energetic. The sermon was to be provoking. We prayed for the altar call to be a life-changing experience. I was nervous and was not sure if anyone would show up, but I trusted God.

The service was a success! The place was full of people. But most importantly, it was filled with the presence of the Lord. Even young people came up for prayer. Everything went well, and I felt that I was fulfilling a God-given assignment of bringing fresh ministry to my hometown.

After a productive worship service, it was on to plan the second Fresh Fire service. The same level of time and effort went into preparing for it. It was the week of and I was busy with balancing work and ministry. I received a disturbing phone call that shook me to my core.

Let me rewind to about 6 months prior. One night, I had a dream that my ex-husband had a child that I didn't know about. When I spoke with him, I told him about the dream. I said, "Do you have a baby? Just tell me the truth." He adamantly denied that he had any children other than our daughter (my stepdaughter). I reminded him of past situations that I dreamed about before they happened. He continued to say that I was wrong this time and that he didn't have any more children.

Now back to the week of the second Fresh Fire service. He called me one night, and I could tell that he wanted to tell me something. He said, "You know that I told you that I would never lie to you again, right?" I didn't know where the conversation was headed, but I knew it was not to a happy place. He said, "Do you remember when you asked me if I had a baby." I replied with a yes. He said, "I just found out that I do have a baby that I didn't know about." The baby was turning one-year-old. According to my math, the child was conceived during the month of our separation. When he should've been fighting for our marriage, he was with a woman that he met while we were still together. Then I asked him if the child was a boy or a girl. When he said, "It's a boy," an indescribable hurt went through me. I quickly told him that I had to go and hung up the phone.

When I was praying, crying, and seeking God to get pregnant, I dreamed of a baby boy. He was cute and chubby. He was in a car seat, and I placed him by my grandmother so she could see him. It was such a vivid dream. It gave me hope. At the moment that I found out about this man-child, my heart sunk. I recall that I cried so hard that it was hard to breathe. I left my bedroom and laid on the couch. I was living in an apartment now so I couldn't scream, but I felt like it. Every negative emotion that I experienced during the marriage was multiplied and cast upon me in that instance. I felt the hurt, pain, disgust, embarrassment, disappointment, anger, and defeat all over again.

After I had gathered myself enough to be able to speak, I called him back. I encouraged him to be there for his child (which I knew he would). I reminded him of the important role that he has as a father. I repeatedly said, "It takes a man to raise a man." He assured me that he wouldn't take his responsibility lightly. I was saying the right thing, but my heart was aching so badly.

Even at work the next day, I carried this burden with me. I was heavy, yet tried to disguise it. After work, I went home and got ready for bed. I prayed that night and asked the Lord to help me. It wasn't a long prayer. It was a quick prayer asking God to give me His joy. I went on to sleep and hoped for a better day.

The next morning, I awakened and something was different. Upon waking up, I knew that the Lord had given me strength. I wasn't feeling heavy and had peace. I was ministry-focused again. It was the week of Fresh Fire, and I had work to do. I couldn't continue going to bed early due to depression. I had Kingdom work to do.

Revelation moment: From situation comes revelation. This statement by Bishop Noel Jones has allowed me to retrospectively analyze and pull out the lesson and blessing from every circumstance. Psalm 30:5 (b) "Weeping may endure for a night, but joy cometh in the morning" was made real to me. I experienced the weeping in the night. I dealt with the distress. Then, the joy of the Lord was bestowed upon me. I am convinced that pain is not permanent. It's difficult to change a person's mind once they've experienced something. I've experienced deliverance from depression, so I'm convinced that God can do it for others. He's healed me which gives me confidence in His ability to heal. Over and over again he's provided for me. Therefore, I'm persuaded that He will always take care of His children.

How did I learn these lessons? Through testing. How do I know that He will take care of you? Through lack. How do I know that he will heal your emotional scars? Through heartache. How am I so sure that he will be there for you? Through loneliness. How did I come out better and stronger? Through CHRIST!

Chapter 8: What's Wrong With Me?

I met a nice young man that asked me out to dinner. I accepted his invitation. From our very first phone conversation, I felt a connection. We had similar backgrounds and relationship struggles. We both dealt with infidelity in marriage. We discussed overcoming heartache and hope for a better future. We had a lot in common, so conversing was seamless.

We checked our calendars and arranged for our first date. He sent me a link to the restaurant's website that he had chosen. I was impressed by his research and preparation for our time together. I was enthusiastic because we were talking quite frequently and I was starting to think that there was something different about him. Something refreshing.

I wore a sleeveless black dress that was flowy at the bottom. He had on a nice button-up shirt and slacks. As we were driving to the restaurant, I glanced over and thought to myself: *he's cute*. He was such a gentleman. He opened the car door and the restaurant door. He pulled out my chair to make sure that I was seated. Again, the discourse was engaging and interesting. He looked at me deep into my eyes and said, "You are so beautiful. I can hardly stand to look at you." I began to blush and at that moment, I felt like the prettiest girl in the whole wide world.

That night sparked something in me that I hadn't felt in a while. His words and the way he lovingly dealt with me made me feel like such a lady. At the end of our time together, we hugged and said our goodbyes. When he left, I knew that this was the beginning of a love story.

Almost every morning after that, I received a "Good morning beautiful," text message. Throughout the day, he would call to see how my day was going. We became best friends. We talked about everything. He said that when we were together that it was like we were in our own world. Every single day he told me how much he loved me. No matter how busy, he always made time for us to spend time together.

He never called me Jessica. It was "Bae" or "Lady J." We installed an app on our phone so that we could see each other when we talked. He told me, "I feel safe with you and I trust you." I knew how he felt because though I was in love before it was different because my trust was perpetually violated. I finally met a man that I could trust. His heart was pure. He loved God. He loved ministry. He loved God's people. He loved his family. He also loved me. Finally, my journey of finding someone that would be faithful to me as I would be to them had led me to him. He was it!

I can be a handful at times, and he was man enough to calm me down. He was gentle enough to put me in my place. He was caring enough to tell me when I was wrong. He was expressive and a communicator like myself. We would talk for hours on the phone when our schedules permitted. This love affair caught me by surprise. I wasn't expecting to fall so deep and so fast. But he was perfect and everything that I had ever prayed for.

His sweetness earned him his own ringtone so I would know that it was him calling. One of my favorite movies is "Dreamgirls." In the movie, there was a song sung that described my feelings for him perfectly. With each phone call, the lyrics rang out…

"Love You I Do"
Jennifer Hudson

Never met a man
Quite like you
Doing all you can
Making my dreams come true

You're strong and you're smart
You've taken my heart
And I'll give you the rest of me too

You're the perfect man for me
I love you I do
Never have I felt
Quite like this
Good about myself

Purpose Revealed

Jessica Smith

From my very first kiss
I'm here when you call
You've got it all
And confidence like I never knew

You're the perfect man for me
I love you I do

You've got the charm
You simply disarm me every time
As long as you drive
I'm along for the ride
Your way
I said it before
There won't be a door
That's closed to us
I'm putting all my trust in you
Cause you, you'll always be true, Oh

I never could have known
This would be,
Oh you and you alone, yeah
Are all for me
I know you're the best
You've passed every test
It's almost too good to be true

You're the perfect man for me
I love you I do
You're the perfect man for me
I love you I do

He shared with me his prayers to God in reference to the woman that was for him. He said, "Bae, you match what God showed me for my life to a T." I was honored that God chose me to stand by his side in life and ministry. I respected everything about him. He was (and still is) a powerful "man of God" with a heart for people.

One day, I cooked us a meal, and we were sitting on the couch after eating. He said, "Bae, I see three kids for us." I was starting to climb the ladder of age and wasn't that excited about three kids. That seemed like a lot. Nevertheless, I embraced it because his words were golden to me. Also, his affirming declaration spoke to my insecurities about my previous infertility issues.

He shared the information with his mother about the three kids, and she sent me a text about it. She was excited. I jokingly told her to prepare to move in because I was going to need help with all of those kids. His family embraced me and were so loving toward me. I was out of state preaching at a revival and his mother texted me "How are you doing, daughter? Just checking on you." I fell in love with not just him, but his family as well.

We planned for marriage. We talked about post-marriage plans often. We decided what city we would live in. He was pastoring so we planned for the ministry and my transition into it. He wanted me to oversee the women's ministry of the church and gave me assignments to prepare for. One night, we were on the phone until 2:00 a.m. discussing strategies to grow and improve the church. It was full speed ahead.

But, there was one major problem. He was still married. His wife left him approximately a year before we met. The divorce papers were drawn up, and she signed them, but that's as far as it had gone. Nothing had been filed.

Pause: I was wrong! Although they were separated, I knew that the divorce was not final. His grounds for divorcing her were Biblically supported, but that did not make our decision to proceed with a romantic relationship correct. I open up and share this portion of my life to teach a lesson. I hope that my mistake is a reminder that the marriage covenant is to be respected. I knew this. I taught this. I was divorced because my ex-husband continually violated the sanctity of marriage. In his mind the marriage was over, but not according to the law. In my mind, the paperwork was just a technicality. I was swept up in a fairytale love affair and didn't pause to really see how the Lord viewed our relationship. Just because it's good, doesn't mean it's God.

Press play: I was at a worship service one night, and the conviction of the Holy Spirit kicked in. As I was sitting there, I thought to myself that our relationship needed to take a break until his divorce was final. I thought about how damaging it could be to ministry. I told the Lord that I was willing to sacrifice because I didn't want to offend Him. I also told the Lord that I needed his blessing on our relationship, and I knew that we didn't have it. I repented and asked God for forgiveness. Now, I had to tell the man that I loved that we had to discontinue our relationship until his status changed.

As I was driving home, I shared what transpired between God and me in the service that I had just left. I told him that we needed to put our relationship on pause. I let him know that I was not trying to date anybody else and was sure about him, but we needed to do what was pleasing unto the Lord. It was not easy, but I've learned that sometimes what right is not what's easy.

He agreed with me and said that he had been feeling that way for a little while now. He proceeded to share his inner thoughts about the situation. While talking, he said, "If I get a divorce." I responded, "Wait! What do you mean about if you get a divorce?" He said that he was in agreement with us taking a break because he needed some time to see what his next move should be. He kept saying, "Bae, I love you," over and over again. This was the beginning of the end. I was floored and crushed… again!

As a result of my divorce, I battled bouts of depression. After the break-up with "him", it was so severe that some days I didn't get out of bed. I lost my best friend.

It felt like a death. I lost motivation. I would dream about him every time I went to sleep. My mind was tormented with memories. My heart ached, but it was worse this time. The sadness and loss of hope affected my day-to-day activities. I hid it as much as possible from my mother and grandmother because they were already ready to kill him. The depression affected my appetite, and I began to lose weight. My grandmother said to me one day, "Don't you lose another pound."

My goddaughter (Tomeka) was by my side the entire time. Some days, I don't know who was hurting the most…her or me. She prayed for me, listened to me cry, and encouraged me. She began to view him as a Father, so she lost someone that she valued as well. I will never forget how she loved me through the darkest season of my life.

I was embarrassed because I was the strong, preacher lady. I was a counselor. I was an advisor. I was a prayer warrior. I was a soldier. How could I allow myself to get to such a low place? How could I be a Christian and be depressed?

A Depressed Christian

Let me pull the cover off of a condition that many Christians attempt to hide. Depression is more common than people care to admit. This is not just something that affects one certain person. Depression does not discriminate. It doesn't matter if you have the most money in the world, you can still be depressed. A Christian can find themselves drowning in depression. So, across the board, there are no boundaries to whom it can affect. It can be a very serious condition that can cause people to be debilitated. It can ruin relationships, cause problems at work, and even make it difficult to overcome serious illnesses. It involves the body, mood, and thoughts. Depression affects the way you eat and sleep. It affects the way you feel about yourself and those around you. One can lose all hope. It is often caused by loneliness, stress, and family or relationship problems. These are just some of the reasons for someone to tail-spin into depression.

In my deepest depression, I would stay in the bed and cry on and off throughout the day. The TV was off, and I wouldn't answer the phone. I felt guilt for being in such a low place. I remember telling the Lord that if he took me in my sleep that I would be ok with that. I just wanted to stop hurting.

People who are depressed or clinically depressed can be suicidal. Some suffer from eating disorders and not wanting to get out of bed or leave their home (which was my experience). They tend to be isolated and insulate themselves, in their pain. It is something that should be taken very seriously. It can really shut someone's life down. People who are depressed cannot simply "pull themselves together" or "just get over it." Depression can last for weeks, months or years, if untreated. Here is what depression looks like or manifests as.

- Persistent sad or anxious mood
- Anger, restlessness, irritability
- Sleeplessness, or not enough sleep
- Reduced appetite and weight loss, or increased appetite and weight gain
- Loss of pleasure and interest in things once enjoyed
- Persistent physical symptoms that don't respond to treatment (such as chronic pain or digestive disorders)
- Difficulty concentrating, remembering or making decisions
- Fatigue or loss of energy
- Feeling guilty, hopeless or worthless
- Thoughts of suicide or death

It is so important not to let these symptoms go untreated. A lot of people are embarrassed by depression, especially if they are someone that leads others. They feel they should have it all together, and publically they do, but privately they are failing. They are not just failing themselves. They are failing all those around them. It can be so mentally overwhelming to someone in the public eye, especially a Christian leader. There is pressure to perform and also to be perfect. It can make it almost impossible for the person to seek proper guidance or help. For Christians, depression can carry an extra heavy weight. It comes in the form of guilt or shame. Since Jesus promises abundant life, Christians often assume that they are not living a Christ-like life if they're depressed. People saying things like, "Have you completely submitted to God?" or "Do you have any unconfessed sin?" do not help at all. I admitted to someone that I had been dealing with depression and he responded, "Don't you know the Bible." It was not what I needed to hear. This type of language just creates a greater shell and hiding place for the depressed believer. These statements carry such baggage and put undue heaviness on the person. They want help but are afraid of being unjustly judged.

It took me a minute to shake it off. Depression's grip is strong. You have to find the "safe place" to admit that you may need help. You don't want to become a statistic. We have to let go of "what people will think." I would rather ask for help, in exchange for suffering. It is critical to know that God cares very much for those who are depressed. That's evident throughout His Word.

Job was depressed. He lost everything, then cursed the day he was born: "Why did I not perish at birth, and die as I came from the womb? I have no peace, no quietness; I have no rest, but only turmoil" (Job 3).

David was depressed: "Be merciful to me, Lord, for I am faint; O Lord, heal me, for my bones are in agony. My soul is in anguish. How long, O Lord, how long? I am worn out from groaning; all night long I flood my bed with weeping and drench my couch with tears" (Psalm 6:2-3, 6).

There are so many other examples, throughout Scripture. The good news is that God hears these cries, and answers. He doubly blessed Job for the rest of his life. (Job 42:12-17). And he comforted David, prompting him to say, "Surely goodness and mercy will follow me all the days of my life, and I will dwell in the house of the Lord forever" (Psalm 23).

For the believer, there are several ways to overcome depression. Number one is prayer and studying the Word of God. Some mornings I would get out of bed and get to my prayer spot in my home and cry out to God. I would tell the Lord just how bad I was hurting. Sometimes I would just sob and ask Him to hold me. One morning, I laid on my floor prostrate and said, "Lord, please heal me and fill me." I looked up scriptures about depression and began to confess them over my life.

You can also seek professional or pastoral counseling. You have to know these sources are acceptable. There is nothing to be ashamed of. Rather than ignoring the depression you feel, face your feelings and ask: "What's going on? How do I feel about it?" and "Do I want to change?" I know that sometimes depression can cause you not to be able to feel. You have to push past your emotions and take a moment to help yourself. Pay attention to what you're thinking about. Don't meditate on your problems, decide to think about what's true, good, right, pure, beautiful, and praiseworthy. Read and meditate on Scripture often to saturate your mind with the right kinds of thoughts. Pray for the Holy Spirit to renew your mind every day. You have to allow yourself to subscribe to Romans 12:2. Be transformed by allowing God to shift and change your mind. Reclaim your mind through the power of God. If a negative thought tries to overtake your mind, replace it with three positive ones. Speak them out loud to yourself and allow you to hear what you believe is possible for you. Refuse to allow your mind to continue to be a battlefield. Ask God to give you His perspective on the relationships and situations in your life that are hurting you. Also, ask God for clarity and wisdom. Correct your vision so you can see them with accuracy. Give yourself permission to stop, think straight, and make better decisions. With God, take back the control of your life and atmosphere. God wants you to prosper and live an exceeding, abundant life. When you give God complete access to you, He can begin to heal you. Believe that, with God's help, you can make significant progress. In a practical sense, as you are healing from depression, get more rest. Stop rushing through your day. Take time to relax. Be a better planner and don't set yourself up for failure. We tend to set ourselves up, by making our expectations too great. Allow yourself to enjoy life.

I'm a witness that you can be a depressed Christian. I've preached powerful sermons and gone home to cry myself to sleep. There were days that I didn't want to live because all around me seemed so bleak and dark. I just wanted the pain to stop. With time, prayer, worship, and scripture meditation, I saw myself come back to life. Yes, I was depressed, but now I'm healed. Since He did it for me, that means He will do it for you.

Rejection is God's Protection

My dating journey has been complex due to the call of God to preach the Gospel. Men would meet me and love my personality. They would watch me minister and found it attractive, yet not know how I would fit into their plans. One guy later admitted that he walked away because he was frightened about dealing with a woman preacher. Another confessed that he was hesitant because I was divorced. It all made me question myself. I wondered: *what's wrong with me.*

Rejection is probably one of the most crippling feelings to deal with. It can be so hurtful to the point many people are handicapped by the feeling of someone not loving or accepting them. When someone reaches out for something: acceptance, approval, the opinion of friends and family—the opinion of anyone at all, a date or request-- there is the risk of rejection from time to time. I can almost guarantee you've had to deal with this, at least a few times in life. I know I have. I've been turned down for jobs that I really wanted. I've felt unwanted in relationships that I thought would flourish. It stings and hurts your heart. It can leave you feeling offended, disappointed and angry. It can even make you feel like a failure. These are all normal feelings under the circumstances! You may have dealt with one or several of the following scenarios which can play a major part in the feeling of rejection. When a relationship fails, the attraction is not mutual, a cheating spouse, love that is not returned, criticism by someone you love and respect that is mean and unfounded, and unwanted sexual or emotional abuse are all common forms of rejection. It makes you question your value or worthiness. It makes you ask yourself, "Why am I not good enough or wanted?" You've possibly wondered if you are attractive enough.

Rejection can trigger an array of emotional, mental and physical issues. It can cause someone to struggle with confidence questions or low self-esteem. In my case, I began to analyze myself which caused me to be extremely critical especially of my physical appearance. So many days, I would look in the mirror and think to myself that perhaps I was alone because I wasn't pretty enough. Even though I lost weight, maybe I was still too big. Was it my acne-prone skin? I felt that there had to be something wrong with me.

The suffering that happens when rejection occurs comes from over-thinking the "loss" that you feel you're suffering, be it the loss of an opportunity, loss of a special relationship, or loss of some other kind. It can be projected onto others because the person is thinking everyone will reject them. They often wait for the next relationship to fail and have trouble trusting or opening up. They may begin to have anxiety when it comes to entering into new relationships. Also, it can lead to eating disorders as they are trying to modify their body due to low self-esteem. Sometimes, the person is so hard on themselves it can cause depression to set in. Honestly, it is frightening to put one's self out there or showing someone who you are and then hearing the two-letter word "NO."

The biggest lesson that I learned from dealing with rejection is not to take things so personally. Our ego is the one that gets triggered by rejection. I had to get my ego in check! It's not all about you. It's not your fault! You have to stop being so harsh to you. There's nothing wrong with you. Sometimes we are not a good fit for a certain person or job. You have to know that God will protect you, as well. As the saying goes, "Rejection is God's protection." It may not be the right timing. There are so many factors that play into why we don't always get what we want. Rest in the knowing that everything is working out for your good.

Allow me to continue to share on the subject of rejection. It doesn't feel good! But don't you allow it to be something you permit to take away happiness from your life. Any kind of rejection, no matter if it's in love, your career, with friends and family, or business ventures. Don't allow it to rob you of your joy. The reality of life is that rejection will form a part of it. There will be times when someone, somewhere will reject your job application, your date request or your ideas for change. For many of us, asking others for what we want scares us to death, because it forces us out of our comfort zone. This is the imaginary place where we have some illusionary idea of being in control. It forces us into a place of not knowing, where we are absolutely out of control. This allows the possibility of rejection.

Let's face it, nobody likes it. As a result, and because the fear of rejection is so strong, there is a tendency for some to sit back, lay low, stay quiet and thus, stay stuck in the box. The key is to remember if you don't ask the answer will always be an automatic no. It is normal to feel bad, so don't try to bottle up your disappointment and sadness. However, don't allow yourself to feel this way for too long because you risk hindering your future endeavors with a negative impression. You still have control. You still have an opportunity to learn from this experience and to approach the future wiser and better. Rejection is a part of life. You have to acknowledge that what really matters is finding the way to bounce back and try again.

There are so many ways to look at rejection as a positive, instead of a negative. What if the person you thought you were supposed to be in a relationship with was abusive and God shut it down? You have to look at the big picture. There are reasons for everything. Sometimes, we really have to reflect and begin to thank God for stopping the process that would have caused us to be delayed or detoured from our destiny. As I reflect on some romantic relationships that didn't work out, I'm grateful. In retrospect, those men were eventually going to be a hindrance to my purpose.

For every no you encounter, there are a thousand more yeses waiting. If you have been terribly hurt in a marriage or relationship, then you really have to take your time and use discernment and wisdom. It is imperative not just to want someone to fill that void or place of "rejection." Don't just have someone in your life to prove that you "still have it." You want to have the right one, not just anyone. The pain of the rejection is sometimes the catalyst for change. It helps you address confidence and self-esteem issues from the past. If you don't feel that you are good enough in your own eyes, how will you be good enough or appeal to someone else? You have to come to a place of self-acceptance. This is an extraordinary experience to realize who you are all over again. You are responsible for loving who God has created you to be. He says that you are fearfully and wonderfully made. You have to see yourself as worthy, whole and complete. This is the other end of the spectrum of rejection. It is really your choice as to whether it breaks you or builds you.

Here are some tips that I've learned on how to overcome rejection:

1. You have to learn how to affirm yourself. Don't wait for someone else to validate your beauty or achievements. Tell yourself that you are worthy, and someone will love and appreciate all you are.

2. Take a moment to breathe. Don't beat yourself up. If you are handed a "no," get up and try again.

3. Don't enter into new relationships anticipating rejection. Let that fear go, so you don't damage a potentially great connection.

4. Remember, rejection is just an illusion and can trick your emotions. The reality is that you are amazing just the way you are.

Understand that you are an asset and not a liability. Within you is greatness! You should pity those that rejected you because they turned away awesomeness. They let a blessing slip right past them. I've discovered that many times what I wanted was not what I needed. I was being shielded from what would not have been good for me down the road. We see the now, but God knows what's to come. Give Him thanks for protection that came via the vehicle of rejection. One day I asked myself the question, "What's wrong with me?" Then I realized the answer…NOTHING!

Chapter 9: The Metamorphosis

"Once I was a caterpillar, now I'm a butterfly; I've been transformed, been reborn, and Jesus is the reason why." I remember hearing this song sung by the Mississippi Children's Choir when I was younger. It sounded good, and I enjoyed singing along to its tune. I didn't know that I would experience my own metaphorical metamorphosis. I went through it to aid others in walking through the different phases of life.

A beautiful butterfly doesn't start out that way. There are four developmental stages. It must go through a process. Egg, larva, pupa, and an adult are the stages, and there is a lesson to be extracted from each of them. Let's look at each stage and pull out revelation for our own life.

Stage 1: The Egg. "A butterfly starts life as a very small, round, oval or cylindrical egg. The coolest thing about butterfly eggs, especially monarch butterfly eggs, is that if you look close enough, you can actually see the tiny caterpillar growing inside of it."

Revelation moment: Everything you need to succeed is already in you. Inside of the egg is the caterpillar. If we take it further, the butterfly is already in the egg also. Inside of an apple tree seed are enough apples for a multitude. I admonish you with words that my Pastor spoke to the congregation recently; it is time to maximize your potential. Recognize that you have the gifting, talent, and ability to be great. Abraham and Sarah had Issac inside of them when they were Abram and Sarai. The Lord promised them that their seed would be so great that they would be innumerable. For years, they weren't able to produce children and tried to help God out by getting Ishmael. God didn't need their help. He just needed their faith and obedience. Even though the odds were against them, Issac was inside of them. Stop depending on others and know that God has inside of you what's necessary for success.

Stage 2: The Larva (Caterpillar) "When the egg finally hatches, most of you would expect for a butterfly to emerge, right? Well, not exactly. In the butterfly's life cycle, there are four stages, and this is only the second stage. Butterfly larvae are actually what we call caterpillars. Caterpillars do not stay in this stage for very long and mostly, in this stage, all they do is eat. When the egg hatches, the caterpillar will start his work and eat the leaf they were born onto. This is really important because the mother butterfly needs to lay her eggs on the type of leaf the caterpillar will eat – each caterpillar type likes only certain types of leaves. Since they are tiny and cannot travel to a new plant, the caterpillar needs to hatch on the kind of leaf it wants to eat."

Purpose Revealed   Jessica Smith

Revelation moment: What you ingest can cause progression or digression. Some of you were mishandled during your caterpillar season. You may have been encouraged to take in things that were more harmful than helpful. The caterpillar eats a certain type of leaf which allows it to grow. Anything that can stop or hinder your growth should be released. Eliminate anything that doesn't produce. Even unfruitful relationships and connections should be removed. If it doesn't cause you to grow, then it has got to go!

Stage 3: Pupa (Chrysalis). "As soon as a caterpillar is done growing and they have reached their full length/weight, they form themselves into a pupa, also known as a chrysalis. Inside of the pupa, the caterpillar is rapidly changing. Now, as most people know, caterpillars are short, stubby and have no wings at all. Within the chrysalis, the old body parts of the caterpillar are undergoing a remarkable transformation, called 'metamorphosis,' to become the beautiful parts that make up the butterfly that will emerge."

Revelation moment: Greatness has the ability to emerge from the darkness. The caterpillar is encased in an outer covering that is formed from itself. It's in a tight place. Although no movement is seen on the outside, there is a change going on inside. If you are in a tight, dark place, it's because you are being transitioned from crawling to flying. The darkness will teach you how to be patient. Have you ever felt like things were just stagnant in your life? Now, you know why. Your butterfly moment is swiftly approaching.

Stage 4: Adult Butterfly. "When the butterfly first emerges from the chrysalis, both of the wings are going to be soft and folded against its body. This is because the butterfly had to fit all its new parts inside of the pupa. As soon as the butterfly has rested after coming out of the chrysalis, it will pump blood into the wings in order to get them working and flapping – then they get to fly. When in the fourth and final stage of their lives, adult butterflies are constantly on the look out to reproduce and when a female lays their eggs on some leaves, the butterfly life cycle will start all over."

Revelation moment: It was all worth it! The hurt, pain, disappointment, and embarrassment made me stronger. Losing my house and cars taught me about restoration. The infertility, broken heart, marriage failure, and the ministry split has equipped me to handle disappointment. Being lied to and lied about gave me experience in the area of forgiveness. Sleepless nights, battling depression, and fear of moving forward allowed me to experience healing and triumph in the midst of obscurity. The loss of employment and insufficiency of money taught me to trust God as my Provider. Again, I repeat that it was worth it. My struggles have groomed me. I'm better and not bitter. It wasn't until after the divorce that my personal ministry began to flourish. It wasn't until after the hurt and rejection that I became sought after for single's events and conferences. Now, I share my story from a healed place and am able to help many. Just like the butterfly that immediately begins to look to reproduce, so do I. It's my intention to facilitate in producing fellow overcomers and conquerors. Say this out loud and say it like you mean it… I ALWAYS WIN!!!

It Didn't Kill Me

Many of us have heard the story of the three little pigs. In the childhood story, it tells of a bad wolf that tries to blow the houses down of each of the pigs. He goes to the first house that is made of straw and says "Little pig, little pig, let me come in." The pig replied, "No no, not by the hair on my chinny chin chin." The wolf exclaims, "Then, I'll huff, and I'll puff, and I'll blow your house in." The wolf was able to blow that house down because of what it was made of. These same series of events transpire at the second house. Again, it's blown down because this one was made of sticks. I can imagine that at this point the wolf's confidence was pretty high because his evil tactics were working. Then he tries the same thing on the third house. He huffs. He puffs. Yet, the house didn't move. Why—because it was made of bricks.

The storms of life will blow, but what you are made of is what determines if you will withstand the winds or not. Time and time again, I've had individuals that hear my story ask me how I made it through. They want to know how I overcame. Most have heard the slogan "Built Ford tough." Well, I was "Built God tough." I know that there is no way that I could've made it without Him. It's because of His healing power that I was healed from depression and rejection. He touched my heart so that I could forgive an offense.

Once safely on shore, we found out that the island was called Malta. ² The islanders showed us unusual kindness. They built a fire and welcomed us all because it was raining and cold. ³ Paul gathered a pile of brushwood and, as he put it on the fire, a viper, driven out by the heat, fastened itself on his hand. ⁴ When the islanders saw the snake hanging from his hand, they said to each other, "This man must be a murderer; for though he escaped from the sea, the goddess Justice has not allowed him to live." ⁵ But Paul shook the snake off into the fire and suffered no ill effects. ⁶ The people expected him to swell up or suddenly fall dead; but after waiting a long time and seeing nothing unusual happen to him, they changed their minds and said he was a god (Acts 28:1-6 NIV).

In Acts 28, Paul and some fellow prisoners have just survived a shipwreck. They land on an island. It's cold and raining. The locals are kind to them and start a fire. Paul gathers sticks to put on the fire, and a venomous snake jumps out and bites him on the hand.

Pause: Attacks often come when you are doing something. If Paul would've been just sitting there, he would not have been bitten. But he also wouldn't have experienced the miracle that we just read about. Be prepared for naysayers when you start making moves. Know that obstacles will come to disturb your focus. Doing nothing disqualifies you from productivity.

Paul suffers a snake bite from a viper. It doesn't just bite him, but it hangs on. This means that the maximum amount of venom was injected into him. There is research and debate about the exact type of snake that bit him. One thing is sure, there should have been some type of negative physiological effect. The islanders said that he should have died. Without medical assistance, he still survived. He suffered no harm. He shook the snake off into the fire. What was meant to kill you, you are going to kill it!

Most of us have suffered some type of figurative snake bite. You may have suffered from an illness that could've taken your life. You may have lost a loved one that could've destroyed your joy. You may have been molested or raped. You may have been in a car accident that should've resulted in death. You might have been so broken that you almost lost your mind. You possibly made bad decisions that were damaging to yourself and those you love. You have lived through it. It was meant to kill you, but it didn't work.

In Order to Grow, I Had to Let it Go

Learning to forgive has allowed me to blossom and mature. Forgiveness is the action or process of pardon, absolution, exoneration, remission or mercy. It is one of the most difficult actions for many people to do. It takes some people years to forgive for one action committed against them. When you forgive, you release the desire to punish someone or yourself for an offense. You can't force it to take place. Just like you can't ignore the process if it is genuine. You have to be willing to deal with and face head-on all of the emotions that accompany forgiveness. There are no short cuts.

Some of the emotional triggers or responses in the process of achieving forgiveness include; anger, torment, bitterness, hatred and self-loathing. It is very easy to harbor feelings of pain and inadequacy after going through a life-altering situation that crushes your spirit. When you are constantly disappointed by the same person or situation, it is easy to lose heart and faith in the ability to see any good outcome. Infidelity, divorce, and lying are a few of the traumatizing events that taught me how to forgive and to move past the pain. It is easy to hold and hide the emotions associated with some grievous offense. The hardest part is seemingly watching someone "get away with it" when there's nothing you can do about it. Yes, your husband or wife cheated on you. Yes, your "friend" sold you out. Yes, they lied to you for months or years. It is understandable to want to scream, cry and be angry, but you can't afford to stay here.

Forgiveness refers to the person doing the action. It is not just about the act. It is to cater and heal the wound of the offended and free the offender. Let me tell you that I have been wounded to my core, but chose to forgive and you have the ability to do the same. If it's possible to discuss the offense with the offender, then this should be considered. If they are truly repentant, then great! If it's healthy to restore the damaged relationship, then you may want to consider it. This is in reference to someone genuine and truly repenting. It may not always include long conversation, but you will know if the "I'm sorry" is truly from the heart or not.

Forgiveness is not trusting. This means that you don't have to run back to your cheating husband or wife. This doesn't mean that you will continue a friendship that has been betrayed. You don't deserve to repeat history or be mistreated again. I chose not to renew some relationships, but I did choose to forgive every person that hurt me. There are instances where you must forgive from a distance. In spite of your feelings, forgive the conscious or unconscious suffering that has been caused. Our desire to be healed from hurt is healthy for both parties involved.

How do I do this?

1. *Acknowledge the person that you are angry with and be honest.* If there are multiple people, start with the one that is the least challenging for you. Allow yourself to accept the fact that you are in a place that you need to issue forgiveness. Be honest with yourself. Once you have accomplished dealing with one person or situation, move on to the others that may be more challenging for you.

2. *Be honest about your true feelings.* Talk to people that are really supportive of you and your situation. Allow yourself to get your anger out. This is not to encourage the act of gossiping! This is to allow a healthy outlet for your feelings and thoughts. Ask for feedback from people in your life that will tell you the truth! Write your feelings down in a journal to release all negativity. At that point, decide if you want to address the person involved or not.

3. *Learn how to forgive.* You have to acknowledge the person you are angry with. This is not necessarily in person. It could be mentally, emotionally and spiritually. Then ask yourself, "Why do I feel like this and what is the main cause of my hurt, anger and/or bitterness?" If you choose to address the person, you want to be clear and direct, because you are seeking compassion for the areas that have caused you the most damage. If you proceed and the person is not ready to treat you as you should be treated or will not acknowledge the action, then you have to be willing to move on without their "personal apology." This is difficult, of course. But, you are well on your way to healing, because you are addressing the point of your pain.

You have to weigh out and prepare for the price of the forgiveness process. Will it cause you more pain? Is it worth the confrontation or intervention? What is your real goal? Is your heart motive pure? Are you looking for affirmation and are they capable of giving it to you? Will you ask without any expectation? These are all heartfelt questions you have to examine before you go into the process. If the outcome is not what you intended, will you be okay? Sometimes, as I stated earlier an apology will never come, but you will have freed yourself from the emotions that have been locked up inside of you. This is a healthy place. It allows you to begin to live again. The offender no longer has the hold on you that they once did. You can begin to enjoy life and embrace peace.

When you enter into forgiveness, a paradigm shift begins to take place in your life. It is a solution for transforming your anger and negative emotions. It frees you from the trap of endless hours of dwelling or thinking about the offense. This allows you to experience more joy and connection. Oftentimes, when there is no forgiveness or letting go, you will find yourself isolating from others. This is done to "protect yourself." But, in the end, you are only hindering your life. Hurt causes us to want to hide away, but you have to be open to loving and trusting again. Not everyone is going to hurt you. Forgiveness does more for you than anyone else because it liberates you from negativity and lets you move forward. Forgiving might not make the angry feelings go completely away immediately, but it will give you the freedom of knowing you are worth so much more. As they say, the best revenge is your success and living in true happiness. You getting revenge on someone that hurt you is never an answer. You know you have truly forgiven someone when you can see them or be in their presence, and the same feelings don't resurface. At this point, you can begin to rejoice, because you are free.

Freedom is the true blessing of forgiveness. You can live, breathe, laugh, and love, and relax. You no longer have anxiety or fear. You don't doubt yourself when you are around the person or people. You have your confidence back. Forgiveness sets you free. Take time right now to evaluate every situation that may have hurt you and begin to let them go one by one. I've experienced this freedom, and it is so liberating. You deserve to be free!

Now I'm a Butterfly!

I'm now the founder of Kingdom Empowerment Ministries whose mission is to "empower a generation of Kingdom Ambassadors." I have the privilege of traveling and teaching God's Word. I often utilize my story to inspire and give hope. I advise and counsel. I pray for and encourage those that are in need. I get to love on God's people.

Daughters of the King Mentorship was announced and launched in February 2016. It is a correspondence program that is designed to help women of various backgrounds. The program has a holistic approach to bettering the whole woman. It is aimed to improve them spiritually, emotionally, professionally, physically, financially and with relational issues.

As I evaluated my life, I received the revelation that perplexities accompany purpose. There was a lesson and a blessing in each and every trial that I faced. Without the adversity, I wouldn't have become an author. The calamity led to me accepting the Call. The loss of employment has launched me into entrepreneurship. Infertility allowed room for me to be a Spiritual Mother to beautiful, amazing children. The loss of my beloved Grandfather taught me the power of prayer. Crying out to God during heartbreak made more evident the anointing on my life. I learned how to persevere in the midst of confusion.

One of my spiritual daughters called me one day. She said, "Ma, why was Joker not able to kill Batman." I replied, "I don't know." She exclaimed, "Because it wasn't in the script." The plot of your life is filled with ups and downs; high mountains and low valleys. But, what God has in store for you is victory! Jeremiah 29:11 states, "For I know the plans I have for you, says the Lord. They are plans for good and not for disaster, to give you a future and a hope." I admonish you to trust Him, love Him, submit to Him, and give Him all of you. I discovered my purpose in the midst of trials and now you will too. Go, walk in purpose!

Author Bio

Jessica Smith is a woman that is making a positive impact for the Kingdom of God. As a minister of the Gospel, she travels and delivers the Word from God in a distinctive and powerful manner. Jessica is a native of Poplarville, MS where growing up she faithfully served in various roles in church such as Youth President. For six years she served as a College Pastor to the students of Grambling State University and later cofounded Ignite Collegiate Ministries. During this time, she served as the Praise & Worship Leader and hosted the yearly "Daughters of the King" conference. Jessica is the founder of Kingdom Empowerment Ministries whose mission is to empower a generation of Kingdom Ambassadors. She established Daughters of the King Mentorship Program to enhance the lives of women of various backgrounds. Her book "Purpose Revealed: Discovering Your Calling in the Midst of Trials" is a journey of her personal struggles and how pain was utilized to pull the cover off of her purpose. She earned a Bachelor's degree in Speech Communication from Louisiana Tech University and has a rich corporate background. She is a servant leader at Life Church under the leadership of Pastor Maize Warren, Jr. in New Orleans, LA. Jessica's favorite statement is "We always win" because she is a firm believer that through the power of Jesus Christ that we are able to overcome anything.